Come Home Laughing

A novel for adult children of divorce

Tanya Lyons

COME HOME LAUGHING

Cover design: Leah Sands

Printed in the United States of America

First Printing, 2017

ISBN 978-1543067569

Printed by CreateSpace, An Amazon.com Company

www.createspace.com

Table of Contents

Author's Note

This story started as part of my master's thesis, but it's been on my heart for a long time. In my own life, as an Adult Child of Divorce (ACOD), I've found there are few resources for adult children of divorce and few places where conversations about the experiences of children of divorce are invited or welcomed. I want to play a small part in changing that.

I want to note that I have written this book from a Christian framework, since that is my faith tradition. I know that for some folks, such material can evoke the pain of past experiences, so if that's you, feel free to decide for yourself if you want to proceed. Keep what helps and discard what doesn't!

In the voices of the various fictional narrators of this novel, and in the carefully selected quotes from sources on the topic, you will encounter some of the emotions, struggles, and heart cries of children of divorce. I believe these cries should be heard, and it is my hope that you the reader might see yourself or people you love here. As you read these stories, you may discover you are not alone in your pain, questions, or fears. I hope you will be encouraged as you read, and that you will be able to find a safe place to share your own story with someone. For those who would like, I have included processing activities and questions at the end of the book.

If you are reading this book as a parent who has divorced, my heart goes out to you, too. As I wrote this book, I thought of you often—perhaps too often. I was conscious of trying not to offend, wanting to protect and shield you, trying to paint a happy picture of the future, for your sake. I'm not sure I was successful. I realize how impossible it is to address every topic is one small book. I'm sure there are many who could write a book to give voice to your pain and your story—and I'd greatly like to read that story.

This story is the other side: the children's story. Yet I hope that in these pages, as a divorced parent, you, too, will encounter the love of God and His boundless compassion for your pain. I hope you will hear His invitation to share your burdens with Him and your story with others. You are not alone in your loss. I don't know the heartache, fear, or loneliness you have carried, but I trust that you love your children. And I ask for your kindness and grace as you read these pages.

For all who are reading this book—I honour you for your courage and openness. To listen to the pain of another requires an open and tender heart, both of which come with a risk and a cost. Thank you for being willing to look at the pain of your own story or those around you. As we pay attention to ourselves and each other with honesty, kindness, and truth, we grow in our ability to love well.

We have a Great Healer who is binding up all our wounds—children and parents—and can lead us into a future of hope and beauty.

Tanya Lyons
Torremolinos, Spain, 2017

Acknowledgements

Thank you to all the children of divorce who took the time and the risk to tell your story in person, over email, or through surveys. It's for you and because of you that I write this book.

Thank you to the editors who helped shape this story: Linda Ardelean, Kay Ben-Avraham, Bobbie Hamm, Vickie Hedgepeth, Donna MacGowan, and Lee Stockburger. Your friendship, expertise, hard work, and encouragement helped make this a reality. I am grateful.

To the staff of the University of the Nations Master of Arts: Christian Formation and Discipleship program, thank you for challenging me to learn and apply what I've been given, and for showing me what it looks like to walk with Holy Spirit.

Thank you to all who have prayed for me during this writing project: Jerri, Paul, Tim, Rita and Randy, Lisa, Jenny, Cindy, Miranda, Gwen, my team in Vancouver, Calvary Baptist in Edmonton, and my Master's cohort. This has been a journey of tears and healing, and I've felt your love along the way.

Divorce is often *the* defining event of our life, and the implications of our parents' choice continue to ripple throughout our life.[1]

Even in instances when divorce was a great gift to one or both parents, it was a silent nightmare to a child. What I am asserting is that divorce—all divorces—leaves major marks on children, marks that reach all the way to the core of their being.[2]

As children of divorce, we fear marriage because we fear divorce, but before we even venture that far, we fear love because we fear failure, betrayal, and the possibility of abandonment... We fear because the risk it takes to be vulnerable and loved means intentionally allowing someone the opportunity to hurt us, and we have already experienced enough hurt to last our lifetime.[3]

[For the child] divorce is a life-transforming experience... Whether the final outcome is good or bad, the whole trajectory of an individual's life is profoundly altered by the divorce experience.[4]

Divorce in childhood creates an enduring identity. Because it typically occurs when a child is young and impressionable and the effects last throughout her growing up years, divorce leaves a permanent stamp. That identity is made up of the childhood fears that you can't shake, despite all the successes and achievements you've made as an adult.[5]

Chapter One

Sunday: Mother's Day

11:18 am

Sloane

The organ music fades as I walk out the front door of the church. Perhaps no one noticed me leave in the middle of the prayer for mothers.

The sunshine seems to say everything is right in the world, but the tightness in my throat disagrees. Clearly the sun has no clue what's been going on behind doors for decades.

Why should I be thankful for mothers? The concept is fine, and sure, I have one, but it would be easier if I didn't.

It never really gets better. Mother's Day after Mother's Day, it's just as brutal. Some years I can't stomach the song and dance at church at all. Better to skip it completely and go to the movies, lose myself in the dark theatre and large fries from McDonald's. My own, beautiful family tradition.

This year, things had felt better. I'd thought I could handle it. I thought I'd grown out of it. *The past is behind me now.* But the panicky feeling comes out of nowhere—the desire to yell and run away.

It feels like there is something with a mind of its own inside me. Unpredictable. Uncontrollable. It keeps me guessing how I'll feel when I wake up every morning.

I wipe my nose and check the time. The service will be over soon. Happy families will pour out. It's so predictable. The mothers will carry a wilting flower. Girls in frilly dresses will show off crafts from Sunday

School and squeal at their brothers' teasing. Fathers will herd children into minivans, opening the door for the flower-carrying wife, recently reminded how fortunate he is to have a woman with whom to share a family: a woman who is a Mother.

The atmosphere will be festive and positive. The cars will drive to lunch at a restaurant. Everyone knows Mothers can't cook on Mother's Day. The extra-lucky ones will head to Grandma's for two generations of motherhood goodness. Puke!

I can't wait for the whole thing to be over.

***

All of us without moms, or whose moms live too far away, linger outside the building. We drink coffee from paper cups while Brad locks up the church and Carole smokes in the parking lot.

We're regulars at Jack's Diner not far from church. Our numbers shrink and expand, but the staff save the corner for us on Sunday at noon.

I end up in the exact middle of a long table, across from Sal, whom I hardly know. I'm eating crêpes with Nutella. She has eggs. Conversations are happening on either side, but instead of joining in, we eat silently.

"I noticed you leave during the flower-handing-out," she says. "You got mother issues, Sloane?"

I wonder how many others noticed me leaving.

"Um, I appreciate a good direct question over lunch, but I'd rather not talk about it," I say at last. Direct answers are not my forte at all.

"Talking about this kind of stuff has been known to help." She says it quietly so no one overhears.

"It's not a big deal," I say, trying to keep it short. "I grew up without a mom, so it's awkward for me. That's all."

"I get the awkward part. Just wait until Father's Day. I'm a mess every year." She rolls her eyes and makes a face like she's choking. "The 'no big deal' part I am curious about, though. I've found losing a parent is a bigger deal than I realized."

I clear my throat and lean forward. "I wouldn't say I 'lost' her." I pause for a sip of coffee. How much explanation will she want before I can change the subject? "She wasn't around. Divorce. That's all. I really don't want to talk about it."

Sal doesn't say anything, and I focus on eating my crêpes. Everyone knows they taste better when they're warm. She picks up her knife and fork. I look up.

"I really like the crêpes here," she says, "and there's nothing quite like chocolate therapy. If you ever change your mind about wanting to talk, I'd be glad to listen."

I can't think of what to say, so I nod—just to let her know I heard the offer.

I hate Mother's Day.

***

It is two weeks later before I see Sal again. The gang is hanging out on the church lawn, waiting for Brad to lock up.

"How's life?" I ask her, squinting at the sun as she sits down next to me. "Frisbee much?" The weather is perfect for Frisbee after lunch. I'm one of the better players and am always looking for people to beef up the competition.

"Not really. Not unless I'm playing with six-year olds." She shrugs and laughs. She looks like someone who would be flocked by kids.

"I'm having some friends over to my place on Friday. I need some guinea pigs for my homemade gelato. Strawberry is the best so far, but I'm branching out into pomegranate and lime. Interested?" she asks.

"Sounds tempting." I do have a fondness for things sweet and fruity, but I'm also fond of keeping my options open. "Let me think about it."

We chat for a while about a new coffee shop close by and when the Farmer's Market will open for the season. Sal's friends give her a nod, and she gets up and brushes off the grass.

"Just so you're not surprised if you decide to come... we all have divorced parents. It's a club, of sorts. It sounds weird, I know, but it's actually cool."

They get together Friday nights to relive the worst experience of their lives? Is that sick, or just sad?

She must have read the expression on my face.

"Does it sound that bad?" She laughs in a way that's contagious. "I thought the same, but when I went, it wasn't too bad. It was alarming how much we had in common. Tragic, but strangely comforting."

Maybe that's comforting to her, but I'm not so sure.

"No pressure," she says. "Doesn't really help to rush these things. If you decide to come, that's awesome. But be warned—I *will* make you eat gelato!" She smiles, and I smile back. The idea of a group eating gelato while talking about divorce strikes me as funny.

She scratches something on a gum wrapper and hands it to me. "My address and number," she says. "Come any time after six." She waves and catches up with her friends standing by the car.

Her invitation is nice, but I can't imagine myself going. Talking about the past doesn't sound useful at all. Why waste energy on things you can't change? But the idea of the group is intriguing. If I could be a fly on that wall…

***

Of course, I skip the group on Friday night. Hanging out with people I don't know and don't trust is not my idea of fun—the curse of the introvert. Plus, I have to catch up on a few episodes of *The Amazing Race*.

***

…children of divorce, even those who appear to be fine and successful later in life, are much more likely than their peers from intact families to share profound and moving stories of confusion, isolation, and suffering.[6]

***

I don't think about Sal or her Friday-night divorce group until I see her at Starbucks Tuesday afternoon. I'm doing a coffee run, and she's a few people in front of me in line. She drops back to stand next to me.

"Sorry I didn't make it on Friday." I pause awkwardly, then offer in explanation, "I had some stuff to do."

"It's not a problem," she says. "It takes time to warm up to something like that." She doesn't seem annoyed. "I didn't tell you much at Jack's the other week, but my parents are divorced too."

"Yeah. I figured that from the support group thing," I say.

"Right, of course you did. Just making sure." The line is moving slowly. She continues, "I was eleven when my dad took off. I told my school friends he'd died in a skiing accident, but I got busted. The teacher called my mom with condolences. Oops. So I stopped talking about it, and nobody ever asked what happened." She pauses and adds, "If he had died, we could have dealt with it, you know? Instead we lived in limbo, never knowing when he'd show up on the doorstep. It was exhausting."

I imagine a small version of Sal waiting by the front door with her overnight bag and school books and unanswered questions.

"I was seven," I say. My voice is totally flat. Seven is the worst number in the world.

"See, that wasn't so hard, was it?" She grins and punches me in the shoulder.

We make it to the front of the line and give our orders.

"Did you know that one quarter of all young adults are children of divorce?" she says. "That's a lot of us!"[7]

"Didn't know that," I answer. We stand in line waiting for our drinks. My order is big, and it takes so long that I feel bad for everyone who has to wait. This isn't a conversation I want to have with an audience.

"You're always welcome to Friday night at my place. You still have the address, right?" she asks.

"Yep, I've got it. Thanks. Bye."

***

...of those young adults who regularly attended a church or synagogue at the time of their parents' divorce, two-thirds say that no one—neither from the clergy nor the congregation—reached out to them.[8]

***

There's nothing quite like finishing work on Friday, the drive home made better by the sky—crystal blue and at least a thousand miles high.

Walking through my front door is like entering a magical kingdom. The stress of the week loses its power, and for two whole days, I am free!

"Hey, Sloane. I'm in here," Meg calls out when she hears the door. Suddenly I remember my roommate is having a group of friends over for a *Lost* marathon. My heart sinks. The thrill of Friday evening and the free weekend disappears. I no longer have a say in my own life or my own house or my own time.

TV marathons mean late nights, groggy mornings, the sink full of dirty dishes, sticky floors, someone sleeping on the couch, and empty toilet paper rolls. Doesn't anyone know how to change a roll of toilet paper?

There's something suffocating about the crowded living room, the odor of popcorn and beer, and the bass of the soundtrack that is impossible to escape. In my room with the door shut and earplugs in, I still feel trapped.

Friday nights are supposed to be fun. So far, these are my options: listening to strangers talk about their dysfunctional families, or hiding in my room to escape a TV marathon. Both sound horrible.

First, a nap. Everything is better after a nap.

I fall on my bed, sinking into the fluffy duvet, and lose myself in the softness of my pillow.

***

The angle of the sun coming in the window tells me I've been sleeping for over an hour. I hear music downstairs. Meg is making dinner for her boyfriend and snacks for tonight.

I smell coconut milk, and my stomach rumbles. It's been a long time since lunch. Meg is a good and generous cook, one of the things I appreciate about her. I brush my teeth to get the nap taste out and comb my straight hair. My face is pillow-lined. No way to pretend I was doing anything but sleeping. Why does it take so long for those lines to fade?

I open the window and push my nose against the screen. The air is clean. I close my eyes and stand there for a few breaths, filling my lungs with something safe.

The gang is coming over soon. I want to get out.

I throw my wrinkly work clothes in a pile and pull on a long-sleeved shirt and running shorts.

Meg and Roger are in the kitchen, sitting on the same side of the table, as newly dating couples do. Any excuse to touch, even when waiting for rice to cook.

"Hey there," Meg says, eyes sparking.

"Hey, Sloane."

"Hey, Roger."

"What are you doing tonight?" she asks. "Sticking around for *Lost*? I'm making wings." Meg knows I'm not a fan but includes me anyway.

I grab an apple and a granola bar. The food smells amazing, but I don't want to crash the love party in the kitchen. "Nah, Sal's having this thing at her place tonight. I'm gonna check it out. Have fun, though. See you later."

My car keys and purse are where I hung them by the door. I take everything I need so I don't have to come back. I don't know where I want to spend the evening. I like keeping my options open. Sal's invitation is a great way to disappear without telling Meg I don't want to be with her friends.

Having an out is the best strategy.

I drive a few blocks to the edge of the park and get out to walk for a while. I love to nap, but it's hard to shake the after-nap headache.

I'm glad Meg found a decent guy. She usually goes for losers who smoke and forget to call. It's painful to watch her waste her time on jerks. Roger seems nice enough.

I'm not supposed to be jealous when good things happen to people I care about, but why doesn't good stuff ever happen to me? What if I'd gone to the lake party with Meg instead of staying home? Would I be sitting at the table with Roger now instead of loitering at the park by myself?

How much of life is pure randomness? Most relationships seem random to me. Couples don't know what they are getting into until it's a done deal. Before long, emotions are tangled, they're an item, and neither person will admit the idea of a relationship is more attractive than the person.

If it's randomness and luck, then I'm the most unlucky person of all. The guys I like always fall for my best friend, or for someone horrible. Anyone but me. I never meet nice guys. I must give off a vibe that says, "Stay away, all of you—very far away!"

I thought Aaron from work might have been interested. He never said so, but there were lots of laughs at lunch and some looks across the office. Then, just today, he tells me he went on a third date with Amanda the day before.

How did I miss that? I could tell him a few things about Amanda that would change his mind. But he's smitten. What's the point, anyway—who wants to be second choice?

They're probably together right now, walking down Broadway, laughing at things that aren't funny. How pathetic.

Actually, I'm what's pathetic. Alone on a Friday night and wishing I was in her place.

Makes me wonder—is there something wrong with the amount of love in the world? The supply seems pretty small, and definitely not enough for my friends and me.

We're all on the hunt for love, trying to find someone who will adore us and stick with us, but does anyone ever get what they're looking for? How is it we're all doing such a crappy job at the thing we want most?

***

But it's in adulthood that children of divorce suffer the most. The impact of divorce hits them most cruelly as they go in search of love, sexual intimacy, and commitment. Their lack of inner images of a man and a woman in a stable relationship and their memories of their parents' failure to sustain the marriage badly hobbles their search, leading them to heartbreak and even despair.[9]

***

I run a few kilometers by the river and loop back to the car. It's close to eight by the time I show up at Sal's. I'm going to walk past the house and make a decision after checking it out. I don't have to go in.

There are other places to go on Friday night—movies and stuff.

I can tell which house it is because the cars are lined up on the street. The open curtains give a great view of the activity inside. I stand and observe. This is even better than I'd hoped—a front-row view to evaluate the situation before making a decision.

The room is full of women, and everyone is talking. I look up and down the street and check my phone. I retie my shoe and send a text to my brother. I'm just a normal person on a sidewalk, not a stalker.

I look again and see only one person is talking now. She's the kind who talks with her hands. It looks intense, but not scary.

I stretch a bit. I walk up the sidewalk. I hesitate to ring the bell; I don't want to interrupt. Can I sneak in? Can I leave without being seen?

Don't be a chicken, Sloane.

I try the handle, and the door opens. I step inside, practically knocking over Sal.

"Sloane, hey, I'm so glad you came!"

"Hi. Thanks. Sorry for interrupting," I whisper.

"You're not interrupting at all," she says. Her voice is a normal volume. "Perfect timing, actually— we're having a break. There's only so long a person can sit still!"

The entry is jammed with shoes and backpacks.

Sal leads me down the hall toward the noisy kitchen.

"I hope you're hungry," she says. The table is loaded with food. My stomach rumbles. The apple and granola bar didn't last long.

"Here's a plate. Eat up. I'm going to get the pies," Sal says, leaving me at the table with an empty plate and a room full of strangers.

Pie is the culinary experiment of the week: family recipes from Sal's Aunt Vickie. There's a lot of laughter as we vote for our favorites. Sal basks in the attention. Everyone fills up a mug of tea or coffee before we head to the living room. I sit on the end of a couch—part of the group, but with an easy exit.

"This is Sloane. She's with us tonight for the first time. I promised her we'd be as unweird as possible."

I'd met everyone in the kitchen, but there were still lots of "welcome"s and "I'm glad you're here"s. It could have been worse.

The room gets quiet, and everyone looks at a gal in a green shirt.

She seems young, maybe still in high school. Her voice is clear as she tells us about growing up in her family and how she feels about what happened to her. There's no way I'd talk like that in a group this big. I hate people looking at me.

She finishes her story, and the women sitting near her hug her, and then one of them prays for her. Sal talks for a few minutes about the human need for connection. We all want to be connected, she says; we need to be connected; but we fear rejection and push people away. We hide the parts of ourselves we're ashamed of, and we end up more isolated and alone than before.

Turns out the gal in the green shirt, Claire, lives a few blocks from me, so I offer her a ride home. She's known Sal since she was a baby and asks if we can stick around to help clean up. I don't mind staying, especially once I remember I'm in no rush to get home. There's a lot to chat about, and those two can *talk*. It's after one by the time we say goodnight to Sal and walk to the car.

"What did you think of our little gang?" she asks as we get in.

"You guys seem pretty nice, and it wasn't as horrible as I imagined," I laugh.

She laughs with me. "Cool. I like those ladies too."

"You did a really great job telling your story," I say. I was impressed with what she said and the way she said it. "I couldn't have done that."

"The first time I told my whole story, I was a mess, but it gets better. This group is great—very easy to talk to." There's no evidence of her tears and no anger in her voice anymore. It's strange to compare the Claire who told her story in the living room with the one in my car bobbing her head to the radio.

We drive the rest of the way without talking. I'm more tired than I realize, even with a nap, and there is plenty to think about.

Claire hesitates before getting out of the car. "Maybe one day, you will want to tell your story, and I'll get to hear it. It's nice to have people who know your story… who know what you've been carrying all your life."

She shuts the door gently since it's so late. "Thanks for the ride!" she whispers through the open window.

"'Night, Claire."

***

When a person tells her story and is truly heard and understood, both she and the listener undergo actual changes in their brain circuitry. They feel a greater sense of emotional and relational connection, decreased anxiety, and greater awareness of and compassion for others' suffering.[10]

23

Chapter Two

Tuesday, 8:14 am

Sal

My brother, Gary, finally agreed to meet for breakfast, so I couldn't cancel, even though I'll be a bit late to work. Gary lives in Vancouver and comes to town every few months for work. Sometimes he makes time for breakfast. Sometimes not.

Gary's late, and I wait, which is normal. I drink as much coffee as I want and think about what I'll say. He drives up in a rental car and parks. He must be on his phone, because I finish another cup and get a refill before he walks in. He looks older than he did at Easter. Tired. Traveling for business is taking its toll.

He gives me a big hug. The man gives excellent hugs. He's chatty, and I don't have to say anything. He talks—hardly taking a breath—about work, his travels, contracts he's signed, the latest upgrades to his condo. The only time he isn't talking is when the waitress gives us the specials.

Fact is, I'm worried about him. His life's bordered on chaotic as long as I can remember. It's amazing he's stuck with one job for an entire year. Girlfriends never last a year.

His roommate, Justin, called me last week. The three of us were inseparable in high school. Justin told me Gary's behind on mortgage payments, and he thinks they could get evicted. Justin transfers the money every month, but it doesn't stay in the bank for long. Neither of us know what's going on. Could it be drugs? Maybe. Gambling? Something else. I worry that the next call I get will be from the police.

Gary is extravagantly long-winded this morning, seeming to forget I'm on a tight schedule. Finally I interrupt, "Gary, something's going on with you... can you just tell me what it is?"

"What are you talking about, sis? Life is great. I just told you about work and my trips. Is it so hard to believe things are going well for me?"

"I'm happy about all that stuff... but Justin told me there are some money troubles."

"Damn Justin! Just has to stick his nose in everything."

"Justin's a good friend, and I'm your friend too, remember? We care about you, Gary."

"I'd pick a different word to describe it."

"You know I'm here for you, right? We've always been there for each other. Hard times are part of the package—there's no shame in it," I say, appealing to our history and hoping he'll open up. "I told you I'm seeing that counselor again, right? Talking to her helps a lot."

"Yeah, whatever works for you, Sal," he says dismissively. "I don't need that stuff, and I don't need you picking at my life. Can't you leave me be—both of you? I don't need your help. Pointing your finger must make you feel better about yourself, is that it?"

"Gary, it's not like that," I explain. "I want you to know you're not alone, no matter what. If you need money or something... I can help."

"Salima," he says, standing up, "I've lived my whole life with a 'rejected' sign on my forehead." He pulls bills from his wallet and drops them on the table. "I don't need one more person, not even you, telling me what I've always known. I don't have time for this." He pulls his coat from the back of the chair and puts it on.

"Gary, you don't have to leave. I'm sorry," I say, reaching out to touch his arm.

"Have a great day," he says and heads for the door.

"I will," I say quietly, but no one is listening.

***

Children of divorce need more time to grow up because they have to accomplish more: they must simultaneously let go of the past and create a mental model for where they are headed, carving their own way... This is far and beyond what most adolescents are expected to achieve.[11]

***

Tuesday, 1:03 pm

Sloane

Later that week, I find myself thinking about Claire and how relaxed and confident she was baring her soul in front of the group. I found out she was twenty, but she looked fifteen and acted thirty.

I'm very different from her. In school, I was so shy. I never spoke, didn't make eye contact, desperately wanted attention, but was terrified of it. Claire, on the other hand, seems self-confident and willing to put herself out there.

I was invisible in school. I never had a boyfriend but always had a crush. I would learn as much about him as possible (without talking to him, of course) and dream of spending time together. If I found out where he lived, I'd walk by, usually on a Saturday. I'd

27

listen for music or signs of life at his house. I'd keep an eye on the windows. When I got to the end of the street, I'd retie my shoelaces and walk past the house again, willing him to see me.

None of the guys were home when I walked by. None of them saw me or came to talk with me.

That scenario is a picture of my life: dreaming and walking and feeling invisible. Always waiting. Hoping to be seen. Longing to be noticed.

I walked down a lot of streets as a kid, past quiet houses and back home again, silent and anonymous.

***

Tuesday, 7:22 pm

Sal has a way of dragging me with her to places I'm not sure I want to be. Very persuasive, she is.

The event is called "Getting a Clearer Picture." It's a series of panel discussions on different topics. In previous months, there was "A Clearer Picture of Depression and Mental Health," and "A Clearer Picture of Cancer."

This month it's about life in divorced families.

How did I live so long without being aware of this underground network? Now everywhere I go, I meet other adult children of divorce. Or at least everywhere Sal takes me.

Signs point to the church basement. Church basements can be scary, but the decorations are nice, and the snack table is inviting. If you're going to get people to spill about their lives to a room full of strangers, there's gotta be some good snacks.

This printout is sitting on each chair:

Getting A Clearer Picture of Life after Divorce

Children in post-divorce families do not, on the whole, look happier, healthier, or more well adjusted, even if one or both parents are happier... studies show that adult children of divorce have more psychological problems than those raised in intact marriages.[12]

For children, divorce is a watershed that permanently alters their lives. The world is newly perceived as a far less reliable, more dangerous place because the closest relationships in their lives can no longer be expected to hold firm.[13]

The question "Where do I belong?" should seem to be relatively easy for a child to answer, especially a young child. But growing up in two worlds plants the question of belonging deep in the moral and spiritual lives of children of divorce.[14]

Tragically, it is well documented that children are at significantly greater risk of abuse after their parents' divorce... anywhere from one-third to one-half—of girls with divorced parents report having been molested or sexually abused as children, most often by their mothers' boyfriends or stepfathers.[15]

...divorce has a "sleeper effect": its worst symptoms often appear when children of divorce leave home and attempt to form intimate relationships and families of their own, but do so with much less ability to trust and little idea of what a lasting marriage looks like.[16]

...it is clear from my work and others that in our divorce culture, the youngest children tend to suffer the most. At an age when they need constant protection and loving nurturance, these young children have parents in turmoil.[17]

In one study, grown children of what might be called "good divorces" (where divorce ends a low-conflict marriage; approximately two-thirds of divorces) often compared poorly even with those who grew up with unhappily married parents.[18]

***

Geoff, the Family Life Pastor, welcomes everyone and explains the idea behind the panel discussion series.[19] He clears his throat. "During my years as a pastor, I've noticed something fascinating happens when we hear people's stories and tell our own. When we listen to someone's pain, it opens our hearts to care about them."

He writes the words *Love* and *Know* at opposite sides of a whiteboard and then connects them with arrows so they form a circle.

"Knowing and loving are connected." He taps and underlines the words for effect. "It's impossible to truly love someone you don't know, but as you know more about a person, love and respect can grow. We've been created to know and to be known. For some of us, this is easy, but for most of us, it's a challenge. Everything within us fights to stay hidden.

"It doesn't matter if you're a high school student, a retired grandma, or a celebrity. We all desperately want to be known, and we also fear it—often at the same time.

"The topics of these panels are important for all of us. They touch the lives of people we love. No home or community is immune to cancer, divorce, or depression. To love others well, we need to know what they have experienced, and hearing their stories gives us the chance to understand at a deeper level.

"I hope these nights will inspire you to educate yourself and to talk about these topics. Hearing from Esther and Craig and Mrs. Brownfield," he gestures to the audience and the panel up front, "puts a face on what we learn in a book, and it strengthens our connections as a community."

He introduces the four adult children of divorce who are on the panel. Their names are written on a tent card in front of them. Alexander is the youngest in the group—early 20s, typical tall-dark-and-handsome with a hipster vibe. Craig is older, late 30s, with a shaved head and athletic build. Hannah is in her late 20s, blond, with a nice manicure. Karen is the oldest in the group: mid-40s.

"Our event tonight will be ninety minutes, with a break for snacks. I have a few questions to get the ball rolling; then I'll open the floor."

I feel nervous for them. What kinds of things will people ask?

The pastor starts by asking each panelist to say how old he or she was at the time of the divorce and what reason they were each given for the break-up.

Hannah starts. "Hi there," she says, giving the audience a small wave. "My parents divorced when I was three. My sisters and I lived with our mom, and we saw our dad at Christmas and all of July. They didn't say why they got divorced. My aunt said Mom hoped the divorce papers would shock Dad into changing his ways, but they had the opposite result. He didn't fight at all; he took the divorce and got the freedom he wanted."

The pastor thanks her for sharing. When she nods, he turns to the next panelist, Alexander.

"My story's complicated," Alexander says. "My parents got divorced when I was eight. Mom married Robert the day after the divorce was finalized. I lived with them for four years, but they got divorced when I was twelve. Then I lived with Dad and his wife and her kids. They had my half-brother and half-sister while I was living with them. They split my first year in University. The reasons they gave... well, working too much, money, unfaithfulness. I think they tried hard, but everyone had so much baggage."

Karen, the next panelist, says, "I was happy when my parents divorced. Mom never explained the reason for the divorce, but Dad was violent toward us, so I'd say that's why. But I missed my dad and wished he'd come back home so we could be together again."

Next is Craig. "I was twelve when my parents split up," he says. "I lived one week at Mom's and one week at Dad's. They said they weren't happy together anymore and needed a fresh start. They said things would be better for everyone if they lived apart."

Pastor Geoff thanks Craig and pauses to read a quote before moving on to the next question:

> As children, we likely were not able to comprehend the difference between our parents not loving each other and not loving us: Why would a daddy who says he loves me choose not to live with me? If Mommy is the center of my world, why am I not the center of hers?[20]

He gives the audience a bit of time to digest, then turns to the panelists again. "Next question," he says. "What do you remember about life before the divorce?"

Hannah starts. "Honestly, I don't remember anything. There are pictures of Mom and Dad holding me as a baby. We look happy, but I had to dream up everything. The idea of having a mom and dad who love each other is a fairy tale for me—something beautiful, but impossible. I wish I remembered those three years, but maybe it's better I don't. It would be too sad."

Alexander starts to speak, then stops and shakes his head. He gestures to Karen to go ahead.

Karen looks down at her hands. "It's hard to say what I remember. It's a blur. I have a memory of going to play on the swings at the park, but to be honest, I've blocked out most of those years. I try not to think much about what it was like back then."

"I remember falling asleep to the sound of Mom and Dad watching TV downstairs," says Craig, when his turn comes. "It was a peaceful feeling to know they were down there together and I was safe upstairs in my bed. After the divorce, the house was so empty and quiet. It felt lonely."

When his last words fade, Pastor Geoff speaks again. "Thanks to each of our panelists for agreeing to share your experiences with us. We're going to break for refreshments, and then we'll open the mic for some Q&A from the audience."

***

Home is the comfort of one shared last name under one shared roof. Home is not made from the extraordinary but from the ordinary. Home is made of countless seemingly meaningless moments of monotony.[21]

***

33

When we reconvene, Sal is the first to go to the microphone. Somehow I'm not surprised. She asks, "How do you think the divorce has shaped your view of love and relationships?"

Hannah looks thoughtful. "Well, it's hard to think about marriage when you grow up without an example. Marriage might be good, but I'm not sure why it's such a big deal. Take it or leave it. Nowadays I'm sticking with singleness. It makes everything easier."

Craig nods. "I can say this… I got married when I was twenty-seven, and I divorced two years later. I knew I had baggage, but I didn't realize it could spoil my marriage. I was shocked when my wife asked for a divorce. I never thought it would happen to me. That was almost a decade ago, and with that and my parents' divorce, I'm not very positive toward marriage. Part of me would like a family, but I'm not sure it will ever happen."

"The jury's still out," Alexander says, "I think relationships are cool, but I don't expect them to last. Maybe the concept of being with one person for your whole life is old-fashioned… not realistic. It's hard to say. When I look at the statistics of marriage, I wonder if it's a thing of the past. I don't think I'd make a very good husband, or father. I like my space and the freedom to do what I want."

Sal thanks them and returns to her seat. Next, a woman with a toddler in her arms asks, "How would you say your parents' divorce impacted you on a personal level?"

"Good question," says Hannah. "As a kid, I had a lot of trouble with nightmares, loneliness, anxiety, depression. There were years I cut a lot. I experimented with drinking and smoking—sometimes to feel better, sometimes to stop feeling. I'm still sorting myself out."

Alexander sits forward. "For me, it's a matter of wondering where I belong... wondering if anyone really wants me. Who would notice if I disappeared? In each of my 'families,' part of me didn't fit. I felt like an outsider no matter where I was. Both homes were full of people, but I didn't feel close to anybody. There was no person in my life who was all mine. I see this in my friendships—I keep work friends and church friends and music friends separate from each other, and I adjust myself to whichever group I'm with at the time."

***

We adjusted ourselves to each of our parents, shaping our habits and beliefs to mimic theirs when we were around them. We often felt like a different person with each of our parents.[22]

The child's very person becomes a confusing reflection of inclusion and exclusion, for he is half of the present parent and half a reminder of a broken, regrettable bond.[23]

***

Karen gestures that she'd like to speak. "It was different for me," she says. "The divorce saved my life. I'm so glad Mom left when she did. We were still poor, and Mom was still unstable, but we survived. We took care of Mom and each other."

A moment of silence passes. Then Craig speaks up. "I'm still figuring it out, and I'm almost forty," he says slowly, "but I'd say the divorce messed with my sense of identity.[24] Let me explain—you take these two people so in love that they vow to be together forever. Those people create another human—that's me—but then something changes, and they don't feel the same love. They break the vow and try to start over again from scratch, but where does that leave me? I'm a permanent reminder of the very thing they want to forget. It's unsettling to think about it that way."

***

With the divorce, the parents have said that they wish this history to no longer be, but the child still needs this history, for she is in the world only because of it.[25]

***

Another woman approaches the mic. "What would you like people to know about divorce?" she asks.

This time, Craig answers first. "Divorce is a different experience for parents and kids," he says. "Parents may get to start over again, but kids never have what we want. The people we love are never together in one place again. Our heart is split in pieces, and it stays that way forever."

Alexander says, "I'd want the kids to know it's not about them. The problems are between the parents. A friend of mine is getting divorced, and when I look at his daughter, it's obvious to me that she is not to blame. But I bet you this girl will grow up feeling bad about herself. Pain will follow her through life, and I hate that. I think people should try really hard not to get divorced, especially if they have kids."

Karen nods. "Yes, sometimes it's necessary. I wish we could make moms and dads love each other… but stuff happens. If you need a divorce, I think you should be able to get one without spending every penny you have. And I think parents should get help from other grownups. Kids don't need to know all the stuff that happened between Mom and Dad. Let the kids be kids."

A guy I recognize as the youth pastor asks, "Can you identify a turning point that helped you deal with the divorce?"

"I can think of one," says Hannah. "I was graduating from University when I realized bitterness and anger were eating me up. Dad had refused to help with my tuition because he'd been 'paying my way' for eighteen years and said it was time I took care of myself. Really, it was his way to get back at Mom for taking him to court over unpaid child support.[26] Anyway, in a moment of clarity, I realized holding on to the past was hurting me. It was stupid to stay angry at my dad's decisions. I signed up for counseling. I forgave."

"Along those lines," says Craig, "my own divorce was a turning point for sure… downward. I was wretched for three years, but then a buddy invited me to live with him and three other guys in a community house. It sounded weird, but I was ready for a change. I've been there five years, and that place has become a real home for me."

"I hit a low point, like Craig did, when I was sixteen," says Karen. "I was drinking, and Mom and I were fighting. She kicked me out. A family heard about my situation and took me in. Their family was so different from what I'd known. The mom and dad and kids liked being together. It took some getting used to. They told me about God, and I went to youth group. People kept on loving me, and slowly things changed for the better."

"Wish I could say the same," Alexander says, looking at the other panelists. "But I can't think of one. Maybe I'm still waiting for a turning point. I'm sure

God and church have had something to do with my healing, but there hasn't been a radical change for me."

***

> Rather, growing up divided between two homes caused many of us to have a less secure sense of home. It often threatened our sense of emotional security and sometimes our physical security as well.[27]

***

Pastor Geoff says there's time for one more question and gives the microphone to a teenage girl, who asks, "What's your relationship like with your parents now?"

"It's pretty complicated, and it's exhausting to keep track of who's talking to who and what everyone is upset about," Alexander says. "My life has enough drama without that. I keep up with my sisters and brothers. If my parents want to contact me, well, they have my number."

"Things with my dad are good," Craig says. "My divorce really drew us together, and he spent a lot of time with me when I was such a wreck. I kinda got my dad back then. My mom passed away a few years ago, and I miss having her around."

Hannah says, "We aren't very close. I call them on birthdays. I've never felt close with my dad, so it's basically a duty thing with him." She breaks off and looks to Karen.

"My relationship with my mom is pretty good," Karen says slowly, "especially now that we live in different provinces. We aren't super close or anything, but I love her, and she's doing pretty well."

The girl who asked the last question returns to her seat as Pastor Geoff walks on stage. He takes the mic from her and thanks her. "It's been such a privilege to hear from you tonight, Hannah, Craig, Karen, and Alexander," he says. "Thank you many times over for your vulnerability and honesty. You have inspired us." There is a hearty round of applause. "To wrap up the evening, can I ask: what was the experience of being on our panel like for you?"

Hannah laughs. "It wasn't as terrifying as I thought it would be. I feel kind of naked, but you all did a really great job of listening, and that made it so much easier. Thank you."

Craig says, "I'm not really sure yet what I think about tonight. I'm glad I did it, but it was weird. I've been hesitant to talk about the past, because I didn't want to embarrass my parents or make them feel worse. This has been a good place to start."

Karen pauses. "I feel a bit sad, because of all that stuff, but mostly because I haven't told anyone this before. I feel sad because I haven't asked my friends to tell me about their lives. It's very special to be listened to so well. Thanks for inviting me, Pastor."

Alexander looks around the room for a moment. "It's a bit surreal," he says. "I've never told this story to a room full of people before, that's for sure. Talking about it can't change the past, but maybe you learned something… I don't know. It was nice to hear the other stories, too. So thanks… and I'm glad it's over!" He and the other panelists all break into laughter.

"Thanks, everyone, for coming out tonight," Pastor Geoff says. "If you can stick around for more snacks, please do. If you have time to thank our panelists, I'm sure it would mean a lot to them. And finally, as a take-away from tonight—consider exchanging life stories with someone you trust. It's a great way to be more fully known and to learn to love more deeply. Have a great evening."

Chapter Three

...peers from divorced families never spontaneously mentioned family suppers or other regular occasions happening after the breakup... Somehow these occasions lacked the symbolic power of belonging to a family, as they did for children in intact families.[28]

Wednesday, 6:14 pm

Sloane

I am on the couch in the living room, chilling out with a well-read book. A summer thunderstorm knocked down a power line and cut the electricity, so a book was my best option. A loud knock on the front door takes me by surprise.

"Sloane. Hi!" Claire yells through the screen door. She is soaked but smiling. Shorts and rubber boots. Huge umbrella.

"Hey there," I call out.

"I'm so glad I got the right house. Your power's out too, right?"

"Sure is. What brings you to this neck of the woods?" I ask as I get off the couch and walk to the door.

"I've come to fetch you for dinner. My uncle barbequed enough burgers for an army. I hope you're hungry. This umbrella is big enough for both of us."

"You don't have to ask me twice," I say. It just wouldn't be right to say no to an offer like that. BBQ burgers in a thunderstorm! The ultimate summer experience. I scribble a note for Meg on the whiteboard by the door and grab my keys as we head into the storm.

COME HOME LAUGHING

***

Even with the umbrella, we're soaked by the time we get to Claire's. From the open patio door I see the table lit by at least a dozen candles. There are cloth napkins at each seat. Not exactly what I imagined for hamburgers during a blackout. I'm out of my league with the candles and fancy table. Is there any way to go back home without offending Claire and her family?

Claire wrestles with the umbrellas and tells me to go inside. I remember her bravery as she told her life story to a room full of people. If she could do that, I can handle one candlelit dinner.

I've never met her aunt and uncle, but they look familiar, as do the other guests gathered for the power-outage BBQ. Soon we are laughing and giddy, like school kids on a snow day. The bottle of wine might have helped with that.

The rain and the circumstances of the meal add something special to the burgers. Since there's nothing else to do, we sit around and continue eating until nothing is left. Aunt Francis takes ice cream out of the freezer—"It would just melt anyway!"—and a pie materializes to go with it. When the power comes on after eleven, Aunt Francis claps her hands and declares, "Well, isn't that perfect timing for some tea!"

***

Dodging the puddles on the walk back home, I think about dinner. It's not that I hate eating; it's that I don't know how to do it with other people around. Spaghetti sauce on your shirt is one thing, but the unknown dynamic of groups of strange people is much worse.

Why so much emphasis on sitting together to consume solids and liquids? Must we gather around a sink to brush our teeth together, or have laundry-folding parties at specific times of day? Do we need an audience and special seating arrangements to put on our socks each morning?

Eating meals together is awkward. The noises people make while eating gross me out. Some people want to talk. Others simply want to eat. It always takes longer than I have planned. The scheduling alone seems like a big task.

Plus, at the table, I'm a captive. If I want food, I must obey the rules and mind the status quo. Eat what they want me to eat, talk about what they want to talk about, laugh when they want me to laugh. Then I have to help clean up a mess that I didn't even make. Waste of time.

Since it's not my home, my kitchen, my decisions, or my family, I have to go with the flow, pass the peas, smile on demand, and remember no one gives a crap if I don't like the food.

***

It's getting the listening you need that makes you strong, not trying to go it alone.[29]

Being listened to creates a sense of being cared for. Not being listened to generates insecurity.[30]

He took Peter, James, and John with him, and he began to be filled with horror and deep distress. He told them, "My soul is crushed with grief to the point of death. Stay here and watch with me." Mark 14:33-34

Friday, 6:08 pm

Sloane

I go to Sal's group the Friday after the BBQ.

Things at work are bad, and I'm looking for a distraction. I'd skipped the other Friday gatherings, not wanting to drag myself off my bed. For some reason, this week, the idea of being around people sounds better.

Sal's one of those people who never locks her front door. "Don't ring the bell—just come on in," she tells me.

I hear male voices in the kitchen. Quick review of what I'm wearing. Passable. Just barely.

Sal introduces her friends from university. Jake's going to grad school in Montreal and is home for the summer. Matt lives in the city.

Has the group become co-ed since last time I was here, or is this an exception for out-of-towners? I'll wait and see.

"What are you going to make us eat tonight?" Jake asks.

"She made you eat stuff, too?" I ask.

"Sure did," Matt chimes in. "We're all guinea pigs in Sal's eyes."

We laugh at Sal's expression.

"You all love my experiments—admit it!" Sal says, pretending to be offended. "Yes, legend has it some experiments turn out better than others, but my record isn't so bad. Make yourselves useful, all of you," Sal commands us, with a wave at the table as she stalks out of the kitchen.

We laugh and eat as we arrange snacks and welcome people as they trickle in. Tonight's creation is fudge—in four different flavours. Sal really has something for sweets.

The first part of the group, which I'd missed last time, is a talk from the Bible. Matt speaks about vulnerability and the inner struggle between wanting to appear capable—like we have it all together—and wanting someone to know how things truly are.

He reads a few verses about the night Jesus was betrayed in the Garden of Gethsemane.[31] Jesus invited His friends to be with Him while He was praying. He wanted Peter, James, and John to be with Him while He bawled like a baby. They kept falling asleep on Him. What rotten friends! I wonder if I'd be the kind of person to fall asleep with a friend blubbering in the corner. What made the story even funnier, if it weren't so sad, was that Jesus kept waking them up.

Jesus didn't drop a casual hint and hope they'd figure it out. He was persistent, and He was incredibly needy. Wanting people with Him didn't mean His relationship with God was weak. Jesus was super close to the Father but still reached out to His friends.

I can't remember ever being so open with my friends. I feel embarrassed when my emotions are overflowing. I think it shows I'm not close enough to God or something.

Matt talks about a time he got dumped by a girlfriend. A few hours after the dumping, a buddy called. For a moment Matt thought about acting like everything was cool, pretending nothing had happened, and crying alone all weekend. His first impulse was to cover up his heartbreak, rawness, and tears.

But during the phone call with his friend, Matt realized he wanted to share life with people who cared about him—and he wanted that more than he wanted to look like he had it all together. He was tired of enduring hard things alone. He took the risk to tell his friend what happened. An hour later, the friend was in his living room, listening to Matt cry and proving vulnerability didn't scare everyone away.

That experience was life-changing for Matt. It revealed a pattern of pulling away from people when he was struggling spiritually or emotionally. Matt believed he had to work through everything alone, that needing help meant he was "unspiritual." "But if Jesus asked His friends for emotional support in a hard time," Matt said, "what's stopping us from doing the same?"

Jesus rejected a lifestyle of "just me and God." He let people see the true Him. He gave and received from others. He lived in emotional and financial vulnerability with a group of trusted friends.

I sit thunderstruck in my seat, thinking what a good message this is. It's not often a guy will talk about crying. We split into groups of three to discuss these questions:

1. When you're struggling, are you more likely to share with people, or to withdraw?
2. When's the last time you cried in front of a friend? What situation brought you to tears? How did it feel to be open and vulnerable?
3. What thoughts or fears keep you from asking for help?

***

This group gets more and more interesting. People spill their guts with one another as if they're talking about buying jeans at the mall. The way they open up the deep parts of themselves, describe intense emotions, and then laugh about something the next second, is amazing. They know how to listen, too—

which is rare. I'm not used to people letting me talk without interrupting.

I don't go very deep with my answers, but it's interesting to hear what Anna and Cassandra say. I wouldn't have guessed the struggles they describe just by looking at them.

We take a break after the discussion. I stay in my spot on the couch and play with my phone while everyone goes to the kitchen for snacks. I hear laughter and yelling. I bet the commotion has to do with Sal and her fudge.

After the break, Sal introduces Jake. She asks him to tell a story from his childhood. Sal describes the power that speaking and listening have in the process of re-wiring our brain. When a person shares a painful memory with a compassionate listener, a new neural pathway is formed in the brain. This pathway makes an association between the negative memory and an experience of acceptance and love. It's a way to escape the trap of shame and fear.[32] I don't understand exactly what she means, but I'll ask her later.

All this soul-baring is unfamiliar to me. What's the etiquette of support groups? Do I look the person in the eye? Stare at the floor? Should I look sad? I'm going to watch what the others are doing.

Jake looks comfortable, but he clears his throat a few times and shuffles his notes.

"Thanks for letting me talk to you," he begins. "I'm going to tell you about something I learned as a kid which kept me from developing healthy relationships as an adult. I learned that people lie. Not everyone, not all the time, but often enough that I began to question everything. People can lie with smiles on their faces or tears in their eyes.

"I learned that the sooner you can accept the fact you don't matter and no one is watching out for you, the better. How you feel, what you want, how another's choices impact you: doesn't matter. 'Take care of yourself, because no one else will' became my motto.

"I learned this by watching my dad, my mom's boyfriends, our relatives, and others. They lied to my siblings and to me. The lies took different forms: claims of love and upcoming visits, lies about money, promising things would be different next time. But utilities got turned off, people left and never came back, and we biked to school in the snow because we didn't have money for gas.

"But let me go back in time to the day before my brother's birthday, when Dad left for the last time. I didn't know it was the last time—he would come and go as he pleased. I should have figured it out, though, because he took his record collection and tools from the garage. We came home from school, and things were missing.

"We were used to him disappearing, but Carl was turning six, and Dad had promised to be there with a present. I thought for sure he'd come back for the party.

"The screeching of the smoke detector woke me up that night. Mom was baking a cake, and it had burned while she was hanging balloons in the hallway. I still remember the smell. Mom hugged me as I stumbled into the kitchen. She made hot chocolate, which I drank silently, while she made another cake. It was white cake, and Carl didn't like white cake.

"You can guess how the rest of the story went. Dad never showed up. We acted like it wasn't a big deal, but it was.

"Birthdays were low key after that. There's only so much disappointment a person can live with. If you don't make a big deal, if you don't have expectations, you don't get disappointed. So I stopped caring. Birthdays, report cards, holidays came and went. Why celebrate when it only reminds you of what you don't have? Better to expect nothing than to hope for something and be disappointed.

"Did the divorce change my life a lot? Yes and no. We lived in the same house and went to the same school. I had a paper route and picked on my little brother. Mom changed. She cried a lot. She worked a lot. When she wasn't working, she was sleeping or drinking coffee in her La-Z-Boy.

"Almost overnight, no one had time for me. I was used to being with Mom—talking, laughing, telling her about school. But she stopped listening. She didn't have time to listen.

"It's interesting Sal mentioned the importance of listening. Listening is a very powerful verb. Underrated, but powerful. When Mom stopped listening, I felt lost. Who was I if no one acknowledged me? Everything felt unreal after that—like I was living in a dream.

"After a while I stopped looking for attention. I stopped asking for help. I'd figure it out myself or learn to live without. Things went like that for years... until high school physics.

"I was in the advanced class, but I was struggling. I didn't have time to study, and I couldn't grasp the ideas. I wasn't used to working for my grades.

"Paulo was a Brazilian exchange student and a genius. Seriously. He offered to tutor me, but of course I said no. He suggested we study together, and I said no to that, too. He got frustrated with me. He told me I'd never figure it out on my own, and everyone realized it except me. He wanted to know why I was so afraid to ask for help, why I was afraid to accept help. They were good questions.

"I was ticked off at being scolded by a guy who could hardly speak English a few months before. But his fluent rebuke gave me something to think about. I was impressed by how much he'd learned. And there weren't many people going out of their way to help me out. The next time he suggested we study together, I agreed.

"I learned so much from Paulo. He made the most of the fact that he was foreign and in a position to be helped. It's easy to like someone you've been able to help. Because of that, he became Mister Popular at our school. I, on the other hand, was cold as ice. I didn't need anything... or anyone. I didn't have many friends. Paulo explained I had a choice—accept help, or be alone.

"He modeled the humility of asking for help. He taught me real relationships go two ways. If you only give or only take, your relationships will never be satisfying.

"And to show you how much I learned from Paulo... could someone please help me by bring the plate of fudge out here? Let's let something else be the centre of attention for a while," Jake says with a laugh. He puts down his notes, and we clap for him.

***

Trust implies a faith that the object of our trust will not let us down. When our parents divorce, we often experience an emotional regression to this first stage of development because the anchor of our security—a home with both parents—has come loose in the storm. The divorce represents a major trust violation...[33]

***

I stay late at Sal's again. Talking with a small group after the gathering is turning into my favorite part.

It's late when I get home, and there's a Facebook message waiting from Claire. She sent it not long after the group was over, but I've been too busy talking to check my phone.

9:37 pm: Hey Sloane. Sorry I
disappeared without letting
you know I didn't need a ride.
I was having a bad night and
didn't want to stick around.
So much of what the guys said
hit me hard. Pls pray for me.

10:29 pm: Hi again. You
must be away from your
phone. I was wondering if
you could read something I
just wrote. I didn't know
what else to do, and writing
helps. It's sort of a
confession or a prayer or
something like that...

12:09 am: Hey Claire.
Just got home
Sorry it was a hard
night ☹
I know what that's like. It stinks.
Praying for you.
I'd be glad to read what you wrote.
Sleep well.

2:33 am: Thanks.
Here it is:
I am such a liar.
I learned early to lie.
To everyone.
I lied to protect myself.
I lied to protect others.
(Did it do them any good?)
I was surprised no one figured
out my lies.
But you only search for truth
if you care about the answer.
And then I forgot why I lied.
I confused real and imaginary.
I imagined a dream world
where I could live.
A dream world where I had
just one home and could stay
there.
A world where the people
who loved me most also loved
each other.
But I got tired of all the lying
and dreaming.
It didn't change things, and it
didn't help me.
So I decided to shut it all
down.
Stop feeling.
Stop dreaming.
Stop talking.
Ignore the outer world. Ignore
the inner world.
Open up to no one about
anything.
But now I'm stuck and frozen.

I don't remember how to
dream.
I don't remember what the
truth feels like.

Chapter Four

Saturday, 10:25 am

Sloane

I'm not The Amazing Sal, but I know there is only one response to a message like that.

I wait until 10 am before texting Claire that I'm picking her up in twenty minutes, and she'd better get her butt out of bed!

Saturday's a popular morning to eat out, and I have to think about where we can have an uninterrupted conversation.

Claire is as subdued as the gray and rainy weather, which makes sense considering how little sleep she had last night.

We don't talk much during the drive, which is fine with me, and I park a few blocks from Zurina's. They have the most amazing muffin platter with the tops of six different muffins and a huge serving of whipped butter. The smell of baking brightens her mood. We laugh as we order.

Claire warms up after a cup of coffee. I do my very best to keep the conversation going. I talk more than normal—giving suggestions about how she could feel better, telling stories from my life, and so on. She doesn't say much, and I wonder what happened to the unrestrained woman who sent me the email last night.

The warm cafe makes us sleepy, and we brave the cold to go for a walk. I've run out of things to say, but Claire perks up a bit, explaining how good it feels to tell someone about her mental wrestling of last night. She's frustrated that the same things keep springing up in her life. "Why can't I leave things in the past and move on?" she wonders.

I don't have an answer for her, but I'm glad I'm not the only one asking those questions.

After I drop her off, I realize I haven't thought about work once all morning—and that's a relief.

***

Saturday, 6:11 pm

It feels good to have people in my life outside of work and my roommate—those are people who have to see me because I'm in their space. Church friends are good, but they're Sunday friends. I like having friends who go out of their way to see me.

I keep thinking about how Claire talked so much at Sal's place and poured out her heart to me online but didn't say much in person. Just when I think I've figured her out, she totally confuses me.

Time to consult the expert.

> 6:14pm Sloane: Hey Sal
> How's your Saturday going?

6:18pm Sal: Cozy and good
I can't believe the
crazy weather today!
How's yours?

> 6:22pm: It's good.
> I took Claire to Zurina's
> this morning
> She was in a weird mood
> Have you talked to her today?

6:32pm: Just a bit
Last night was hard for her
but nothing out of the ordinary
Why?

6:35pm: I thought she wanted to talk
but she didn't say much
I had to do all of the talking

6:37pm: That's interesting.
Are you normally the
talky type?

6:38pm: No way
I'm a listener

6:38pm: Yet you did most
of the talking?

6:40pm: Yeah, and it wasn't easy
to keep the conversation going
I had to ask a zillion questions!

6:41pm: And when she
didn't answer...?

6:42pm: I told her stories from
my life, encouraging
quotes from church...
It was awkward

6:43pm: Man, that's funny!

6:44pm: Funny????

6:45pm: Sorry...
I can imagine... Claire half asleep
trying to think about deep stuff
You, in a very un-Sloane-like
manner pulling out every Hallmark
slogan and sappy story you can think of

6:49pm: Sappy!!!
Come on...
What was I supposed to do?

6:50pm: Oh honey, don't get me wrong
You did so many things right!
You showed up, you cared
You took her to Zurina's!

Gosh, you're a great friend!

6:52pm: So…
what did I do wrong?

6:54pm: I'll email you an
article about listening.
Take a look and tell me
what you think…

6:56pm: K

7:01pm: Done! It's on its way
You are a good friend, Sloane
I think it means a lot that Claire
trusted you with what was going on
I gotta run.
Ttyl!

7:03pm: Thanks for sending that. Later.

I'm curious to read this article about listening. I'm a great listener (I think; I thought), but maybe there's more to learn.

Twenty minutes and two readings of the article later, I can admit I basically did everything wrong.

I discounted Claire's feelings (Oh, come on—don't feel that way, it's not so bad). I was pushy (Why are you so quiet? Tell me what's going on!). I made it about me and told a bunch of stories from my life (I've had lots of hard times too. There was this one time…). Her body language alone should have been a huge clue.

I'm an idiot. No wonder Sal was laughing at me.

I write out a few pointers about how to be a good listener for future reference:

- Space to think is important. The deeper the issue, the more time is needed.

- Shut up and listen. Let the person talk, even if what they say is illogical, a downer, or uncomfortable to hear. (Just stop talking!)
- Pay attention. Don't interrupt. Put the phone away. Don't fiddle.
- Silence is not the enemy. (Count to ten before asking another question.)

I need to go for a run to let it all sink in.

Around three kilometers in, I realize what I'm feeling is irritation. It's that familiar feeling of not knowing what I'm supposed to do. Despite my good intentions, I probably made things worse for Claire. I was supposed to help her, but I made her life harder.

For a long time after Mom left, no one knew what we were supposed to do. During the day we went through the motions, but everything felt different. It was as awkward as trying to write left-handed—readable, but wobbly.

Laundry and pigtails for soccer practice didn't look as good as before. We learned over time, but getting good at the pieces of life meant she wasn't coming back. We didn't want to admit life without her was permanent.

That year when Halloween was coming up, we agreed to skip it. Mom was the one who'd made a big deal about dressing up. She'd start working on costumes as soon as school began in September.

I couldn't imagine Dad trying to do all that. Andrew and I talked about it first and then told Mary. She held back tears and nodded in agreement. Andrew and I told Dad we were too big to dress up, and Mary's school was banning Halloween.

Whether he believed us or not, he agreed we'd let it go that year. Mary was brave and nodded in all the right places. I gave her an extra big hug. It was for Dad she held back her tears.

We made chicken nuggets and popcorn for dinner on Halloween and ate downstairs so no one could tell we were home.

Dad brought a big bag of candy home after work with him. After dinner we split it between the three of us. It was never so easy to get Halloween candy! We didn't have to walk in the cold, wondering which houses had the best treats. All we needed was a mom to walk out and a dad willing to comfort us with bite-sized chocolates.

Chapter Five

Tuesday, 7:18 pm

Sloane

This week's been horrible from the get-go. Why can't I have a happy, normal life like everyone else? I go to bed each night with a tight stomach. The early morning semi-conscious moments when I can't remember what's going on are the best part of my day.

As soon as I'm actually awake, it hits me. Nothing has changed. Things are horrible. I hate my life.

I drag myself through seventeen hours and do it all over again.

The highlight of the week was when Sal dropped by with ice cream bars.

I'm not used to having someone like Sal in my life—in my face. Honest and extremely persistent. The woman is a bloodhound—friendly but ruthless. Maybe a bloodhound crossed with a golden retriever.

I've gotten used to her messages and surprise visits and her open-door policy. Pretty soon she'll be handing out keys to her front door!

She had news to share with the ice cream. Someone pulled out of the retreat in Banff, and there's room for me to go. I've heard a few chats at church about a trip to the Rockies. Sounded cool. Now I know some of the people going, I'm jealous they get to spend a week in the mountains. I don't remember my last vacation.

I'm touched she thought of me, but there's no way to get time off work. The idea of asking my boss for a favor makes me want to throw up. I'm trying to stay relaxed and positive about life at the office—but it's not easy.

Sal knows things aren't going well, but I haven't given details. It's better that way. Plus, I feel like a loser when I talk about it.

We spent an hour streaming music videos and band clips online. Sal has good taste in music. One of her roommates works at a record store. Their house is full of demo tapes and indie posters.

I told her I can't go, but she says she's going to pray something will work out.

Pray all you want, I think. *If God wants to use up a miracle for this, He's welcome.*

***

Wednesday

> 5:43pm Sloane: Hey Sal.
> How are ya?

5:45pm Sal: Hey Sloane.
I'm good

> 5:45pm: I finally found the song
> I was talking about. Search "Wake" by Hillsong
> United, on YouTube.

5:46pm: Sweet
Gimme a few minutes to listen to it

5:52pm: Just heard it. Beautiful!

> 5:53pm: Yeah
> and annoying

5:54pm: Annoying?

> 5:55pm: Yes, because I haven't
> experienced love like that
> Did you hear these lyrics:

"You will never fade away
Your love is here to stay
By my side
In my life
Shining through me every day…
You're in my heart forever"

5:58pm: ☹

5:58pm: People say they love me
but it always fades
They don't stick around:
Parents
Guys
Friends
…will I ever be loved like this?
Is it even possible…?

6:02pm: Tough question, friend
Some people say,
"Yes, of course"
But I can't give you a guarantee
We all want love like that
someone to depend on

6:05pm: Do you have someone
like that in your life?

6:05pm: If God counts, then yes

6:06pm: Haha—yes, He counts.
But what does it even mean
to have Him in your life like that?
You can't see Him or touch Him

6:08pm: Very true.
It is kind of ridiculous
to have an invisible friend
as a grown-up
But… there's something I learned
in human development class
that helped me
You want to hear it?

6:10pm: Sure

6:11pm: It's called
"emotional memory"[34]

6:11pm: Go on

6:12pm: When babies are growing
up they learn about the world
and people through experience
They have a very short
memory though

6:13pm: Got it

6:14pm: So, it takes a while to
figure out what's going on and
make sense of the world.
They can't communicate (apart from
crying)
They are vulnerable and dependent
Over time they realize certain
people take care of them
These people feed/change/comfort
them. The people appear and
disappear, but gradually they learn the same
people stick around
The baby learns the voice and
smell of Mom/Dad/Grammy
When that person is around
the baby feels safe

6:19pm: The baby connects
Mom/Dad/Grammy
with safety and security

6:20pm: Yes
And when the kid is
dropped off at the nursery
he acts like the world is ending!

6:21pm: So true!
He's like, everything I know and trust
just walked out the door!

6:21pm: Without that person around, life is scary
Anyway, this is an important
developmental step for the baby...
making a connection between
the caregiver and safety
The next step is when the baby starts
to remember Mom/Dad/Grammy
even when that person isn't there
The baby has enough memories to feel secure
The image of the parent has become
strong in the baby's mind.

6:26pm: The idea of mom or dad
is stored in his long-term memory

6:27: Yeah. It's been written in
his hard-drive
He doesn't freak out or panic
He's secure
That's the emotional memory
It impacts the kid's feelings and actions

6:29pm: OK. Got it.

6:30pm: It might not be exactly the same
but I noticed my emotional memory
was fragile, wimpy
I'd freak out every time
something went wrong

6:34pm: Like the kid
in the nursery wondering
"will they come back
for me this time?"

6:35pm: Yeah. Instead of feeling
relaxed and peaceful

I was nervous about everything
I expected I'd be forgotten

                          6:38pm: That stinks, and I get it.

6:40pm: So I learned to take control
and not depend on anyone

                        6:42pm: Yep, I know that feeling.
                        But how is this connected to God?
6:43pm: Bear with me.
It's connected.
                        6:43pm: Thought so

6:44pm: I don't expect my
parents to be there for me anymore
I'm an adult
but there was the question…
Who can I trust?
Who can I depend on?
People told me following God
would fix everything,
but that was a lie
                        6:46pm: A Christian lied to you!!!?
                        I can't believe it!
6:47pm: Haha—yeah, they did
We know following God
makes life MORE complicated
                        6:48pm: True
6:46pm: Anyway, I realized
I needed something to hold onto
I needed to build an emotional memory
that was deeper than memorized Bible verses
and happy quotes about "God's love" and
"everything happens for a reason"

6:49pm: Oh, sorry to do this
but I just noticed I'm going to be
late for Ultimate if I don't jet

6:50pm: Sure, no prob

6:51pm: let's talk later—
I want to hear the rest of it

6:52pm: Sure thing. Have fun!

6:52pm: Bye

***

The entire first year of life is ideally built around helping the infant to take in, or internalize, this sense of belonging and safety. Internalization takes thousands of experiences of the parents' being there for the infant when he needs them. This is because we are creatures of memory. God gives us memory to help us understand the world and avoid mistakes.[35]

Chapter Six

Saturday

3:14pm Sloane: Hey again.
How are ya?

3:15pm Sal: Hey there—I'm good
Who won your game Wednesday?

3:16pm: Not us
We got crushed ☹
Sorry I had to run—you
were getting interesting

3:18pm: Haha.
I can get preachy.

3:19pm: Nah—you weren't preaching
Have time now to
finish your "sermon"?

3:19pm: Sure do.
Where were we?

3:20pm: Emotional memory
Babies learn to trust
because they remember
their parents being there
for them

3:21pm: Right-o

3:22pm: You were going to explain
the connection to God

3:23pm: Yes, I was. Let's see…
Emotional memory has two parts
Part 1: EMOTIONS

3:23pm: Makes sense

3:23pm: To have a healthy emotional
memory, you need more than facts
There have to be feelings connected
to the actions

I was not a big fan of emotions
I thought they were more trouble
than they were worth

                    3:26pm: Yes. agreed

3:27pm: However, they are important
and you can't deny them forever
(I tried)

                    3:29 pm: If you say so

3:30 pm: Part 2: MEMORY
There needs to be history,
some kind of story
to hold it all together
The memories gradually
build up over time

          3:31pm: And some memories
          stick with you for a long time!

3:31pm: Yes, so true
To strengthen my emotional
memory with God I made a timeline
of our life together,
something I could look at
to represent what
I wanted to build on the inside—
the times when I experienced
God's presence and involvement
I spent a week looking over my life
I used photo albums, journals,
old calendars, FB

                    3:35pm: Sounds exhausting

3:35pm: Yeah, it was
but I was shocked by the stuff
I found!
God had done way more in my life
than I gave Him credit for

3:36pm: Nice

3:37pm: It takes a baby years
to learn security and I needed
a LOT of experiences
with God to build that same
secure memory because I had
a lot of negative experiences to combat.
The emotional stuff was strange
territory for me, but I did it.
You still there?

3:40pm: Yep. Tracking.

3:40pm: Just let me know if
you need to go—
I can get carried away

3:41pm: Gee—I hadn't noticed ☺
But seriously, this is good
and I have time
Keep going

3:43pm: I made a list of times
I'd felt His love
moments He felt close to me
experiences that communicated
I was loved and I belonged to him

3:45pm: You wrote it all out??

3:45pm: I made bullet points:
Starry night at summer camp…
On the grass outside Aunt Sara's…
Margaret's prayer at Christmas party….
Conversation with Larry in the garage…
and so on
I hung the list on the wall next to
my desk so I could see it.

I still look at it when I feel
anxious or worried
I hold on to what I've experienced
in the past to remind myself
God is trustworthy

> 3:50pm: That sounds cool.
> I thought it was going to be
> way more complicated

3:51pm: Sound like something
you'd ever do?

> 3:51pm: I don't know
> I don't think I have
> many things to write down

3:54pm: Yeah, I hear what
you're saying.
That could make it difficult…

> 3:57pm: But…?

3:58pm: It might not be as hard
as you think. When you look for
God's love you start seeing it

> 4:00pm: I'll think about it

4:00pm: That's great
Hey, are you sure you can't
come to the retreat?

> 4:02pm: I wish I could,
> but it's not going to work out
> Hey, I have some stuff to do
> around here so I'm gonna go

4:04pm: Ok, away you go.
See you at church tomorrow!

> 4:05pm: Yep. See ya!

***

I remember a conversation I had with Nathan, my ex-boyfriend, while we were dating. The relationship didn't last long, because it was just one drama after another.

After one fight, when the dust had settled, he asked if I realized how sensitive I was. He commented that really small things would set me off, and once I got upset, I acted like the relationship was basically over. He said it was exhausting to be with someone who blew small things up into huge problems.

Dude didn't realize he was calling out my pathetic "emotional memory." I couldn't admit it at the time, but I often freaked out over small things. If a person would hurt me in a small way, why would I trust him with something bigger? It sounded logical to me.

If I think about it from his perspective, I see how difficult it would have been to date me—always wondering when I'd wig out, constantly having to defend against my fear and insecurity. No one wants to date someone with the emotional maturity of a child. Seriously, relationships are complicated!

***

The children concluded early on, silently and sadly, that family relationships are fragile and that the tie between a man and woman can break capriciously, without warning... These early experiences colored their later expectations.[36]

Many of us stuff our feelings of betrayal, rejection, fear, anger, and abandonment. In the backs of our minds, we consoled ourselves with the hope that things would get better when we were on our own... As we seek our own romantic relationships, we discover we don't know how to create what we desire, and the fear that we'll re-create what we've left behind consumes us.[37]

Chapter Seven

Saturday, 7:13 pm

Sal

To: m.l.fitzgerald@uoftg.edu
From: spdickensfield@qtmail.com
Subject: How to summarize emotional memory and attachment theory

Dear Professor Fitzgerald,

I hope you are doing well and enjoying your summer in Ireland. I won't tell you about the great weather we're having here (my mother taught me not to brag, and definitely not about things I can't take credit for). Thanks again for your offer to answer questions about the content from the past semester. I learned so much from your lectures, and I'm glad you were able to spend the year with us in Saskatoon.

I've been talking with a friend recently, trying to explain emotional memory and attachment theory. She has no foundation in the field, and I'm not sure how to help her without overwhelming her. If you only had a page or two, what would you say to a person who wants to develop secure attachment?

Not all professors are comfortable giving advice so informally, but many times you said there's no point to what we know if we can't give it to those who truly need it. In my estimation, this friend could benefit greatly from some applied understanding in this area.

Thanks in advance for your insights and suggestions.

Sincerely,
Salima Dickensfield

P.S. My friend shares our faith and loves the One we love.

Tuesday, 4:03 am

To: spdickensfield@qtmail.com
From: m.l.fitzgerald@uoftg.edu
Subject: Re: Summary of emotional memory and attachment theory

Dear Salima,

Thanks for your message. Yes, indeed, all it takes is a brief look at the weather channel to wonder why I left Canada for Ireland in summer!

I'm glad you found someone who will listen to you talk about what we discussed this past semester. A live audience forces one to adjust your delivery and tailor content to what will be of greatest benefit.

Am I correct to believe your friend experienced some trauma as a child? By *trauma*, I refer to an event which interrupted her ability to experience the world as a safe, trustworthy place. Perhaps now as an adult, she feels stuck in unsatisfying relationships and unable to identify necessary changes.

Don't underestimate your comprehension of the material and your ability to evaluate what would help her—you were a very good student! However, because you have asked for input, I will share some thoughts.

I would begin by explaining the concept of attachment (the deep desire to connect with others) and how a child's experience of attaching (or not) to a primary caregiver shapes the brain's neural networks. (In case she isn't familiar with neuroscience, refer her to Dr. Thompson's *Anatomy of the Soul.*[38]) The way one learned to manage his/her emotional state as a child will follow him/her into adult friendships, marriages, and work relationships.[39]

The goal is a "secure attachment," where a person operates from a place of security and is able to venture into the world without fear.[40] What you experience as a child *has* shaped you. These fundamental ways of relating will *not* change, without significant influence from an outside relationship or a dramatic shift in circumstance.[41] A person's pattern of relating actually becomes *more* solid over time (at a neurological level). The good news is that it's possible for attachment patterns to be altered. With God involved, there is so much hope for transformation.

You could describe different types of insecure attachment (avoidant, ambivalent/anxious, and disordered) and their general characteristics. (There are some wonderful YouTube videos about these.) Insecure attachments are common where parents were emotionally unavailable, care was inconsistent, or in homes marked by chaos. These children often disconnect emotionally or lean toward a rational, left-brain approach in order to cope with an unpredictable and treacherous world.

As you will recall from lectures, acquiring the desired "earned secure attachment" does not happen quickly. It takes *work* to change such well-developed neural pathways.[42] In situations where a patient desires to move to a secure attachment, I have witnessed God Himself helping this transformation at the level of thoughts, emotions, and healing of memories. Truly there is no part of us He does not care about!

I imagine by this point your friend will have a lot to digest, and she may contact the administration to request partial credit for my course! Because of the complexity of this topic, simply identifying her attachment style may provide much for her to chew on. From there, after she's had sufficient time to think, you could talk about steps forward. Be sure to remind her as often as necessary that she is not alone in this process of change and transformation. God is closer than our breath, and He knows how He created us. There is great hope for her to develop a greater sense of internal security and greater connection in her relationships.

All the best as you give away what you've been given,
Marguerite Fitzgerald

***

Sunday, 2:41 pm

Sloane

> I fear that divorce has become so common in our culture that those of us who lead and participate in religious communities have stopped *seeing* it. Like violence on TV... our

unwillingness to see due to over-exposure communicates that the issue is not a big deal, that it is normal, that it is common to feel your very being stripped from within you.[43]

***

Church was good today, though I don't remember much of the sermon. I was too busy trying to forget tomorrow's Monday. Maybe a cigarette with Carole out back would calm my nerves.

Jake invites the gang to his mom's place for lunch, and I say yes. I don't have much food in my fridge. The diner will have to survive without us this week.

Jake and Matt know everyone, so lunch is a reunion of sorts. Big groups are okay if I know the people, and this group is a combo of Sal's support group and church.

Turns out a lot of them are going to the retreat. When they start talking about the hikes they want to do on the way, I head for the kitchen.

Jake's mom is *puttering*, as my dad would say. She looks too young to be anyone's mom, but I see the family resemblance.

Something about being in a sunny kitchen puts me at ease. I find myself sitting on a bar stool, telling her about everything at work: the written warning, the discipline letter, the sick feeling I get in my stomach every time two particular coworkers come near my desk. She asks if I have people I can talk to about it. I tell her no, and she doesn't say anything to fix me. She gives me a hug and pats my hair. I'm not used to a mother's touch, and it's not until later I realize how I've missed it.

"It's nice to have Jake home, even for the summer," she says when the conversation turns. "He's grown into a quality young man—which is a relief. There were years when it was touch and go. It's a miracle I have any hair left on this head of mine!"

I wonder what it was like for her, raising Jake and his brothers as a single mom. I wonder if this is the kitchen where Jake drank hot chocolate while she baked the birthday cake at midnight.

"Can I ask you something?" I say.

"Yeah, sure." She pauses from wiping the counter and looks at me.

"Have you been able to forgive your husband… ex-husband… for what he did?" All the talk about feelings and the past gives me a new boldness.

"Yes, I did," she says quietly. "It took me a very long time, though. First I had to find a way to let go of my anger. For years, anger was the only thing I felt. It was the fuel getting me out of bed in the morning.

"Then, one day, I was at the sink, doing dishes. I looked over my shoulder to check on Jake in the other room, and with a shock I realized it wasn't Jake—it was his brother Sammy, who is seven years younger. Seven years had passed without me noticing much of anything! Those years had disappeared. I decided then and there that something needed to change.

"I found a support group, and that really helped. Being around people who understood the pain of a destroyed marriage broke up the dark cloud hovering over me. The group became a family for us, and we're still close."

I wait a few moments and say, "Thanks for telling me," just like Sal taught us at her group. I'm grateful to hear a first-hand story about forgiveness, since I haven't heard many.

"Do you have any people you need to forgive?" she asks.

I nod.

"When the time is right, you will," she says and gives me another hug. "How about we see if the gang needs more provisions? I know how much those boys can eat!"

She sends me downstairs with a platter of watermelon, and I help them devour it as they make final plans for the trip to Banff. I offer to loan my camping supplies, since I won't need them that weekend. I don't really want to go, but I feel the familiar sting of being left out, nevertheless.

***

...what the child needs is not a zone of happiness, but a community of shared being, a community to be-with that is powerfully responsible for his or her being-in-the-world.[44]

Chapter Eight

Wednesday, 5:14 pm

Sloane

"Sloane, are you home? Open up; it's Sal."

I'm upstairs in bed but hear her calling out through the screen door downstairs. People who drop by without any warning are annoying.

"Sloane, I'm pretty sure you're here, since your car's out front and I can see your purse by the door. Are you okay?"

Must hide purse next time I don't want people to know I'm home.

"I'm here to pick up the camping stuff. Open up."

I can hear her trying to open the locked screen door.

The woman is not going to go away.

I get out of bed and grab the camping stuff from the pile on my floor.

Sal's waiting outside the door, checking her phone.

"You didn't respond to my text. Did you lose your phone?" she asks when she sees me coming down the stairs.

I open the door and let her in.

"Oh, no. What's wrong?" she asks when she sees my face.

"I got fired." My voice is a whisper.

"Ohhhhh," she says and takes the sleeping mat and camp stove from my hands. "Come and sit down."

She leads me to a seat in the kitchen and puts the kettle on. At some point, a mug of peppermint tea appears. Sal is sitting across from me, waiting.

"Can you tell me what happened?" she asks.

"I... I... I didn't expect this. I mean, things weren't good, but I didn't think they'd fire me. I've been there for years. I was going to make it work." I'm crying again. Sal hands me Kleenex.

I've been crying and swearing and throwing things since they sent me home this morning. How could they fire me? I should've quit, but I simply didn't see it coming.

"They told me it wasn't 'working out,' and they had to 'let me go,'" I say, making quotations marks in the air. "Why do they say it that way? 'Let me go.' As if! They aren't 'letting me' do anything. They're kicking my butt to the curb! Good riddance to them— bunch of selfish, stuck-up losers!"

I'm crying again.

Sal keeps giving me tea and glasses of water. Eventually she decides I need food.

"Go change your clothes, Sunshine." Calm and in charge, like usual. "Wash your face," she says. "We're going for a cheeseburger."

"I don't want a cheeseburger," I say. "I'm not hungry."

"Fine, you don't have to eat anything, but I need a cheeseburger."

***

I avoid looking in the mirror as I wash my face and brush my teeth. I'm definitely wearing sweat pants... and a hat.

Over a cheeseburger, which I eat (of course), I tell Sal the whole drama of work over the past years. My struggle with inappropriate outbursts. The anger issues. The reprimands and the warning letter. The tension in the office. The co-workers' provocations and taunts. My attempts to keep everything under control. My failure at everything.

We eat dessert too—pie *and* ice cream. I don't taste any of it, but I eat because it makes Sal happy.

I feel like crap.

Sal drops me off and promises to check on me tomorrow.

"The silver lining here, my friend, is now you can come to the retreat with the rest of us." Is she smiling as she says that?

"I'm not going anywhere." I'm sulking and so tired. "I'm sure the space is taken. Plus, there's no way I can afford something like that now."

"You are most definitely going. I happen to know there is room for you. And don't worry about the cost of the week, it's covered," she yells out the window as she drives away.

That woman!

***

Friday, 6:18 pm

I haven't seen a lot of Meg and Roger in the past weeks. I've been spending more time with Sal and her friends, and our schedules don't cross much. I enjoy Meg, but Roger has been getting on my nerves. He's one of those people who thinks he's right about everything.

I take a break from packing to eat Thai take-out with them in the backyard. Roger is curious about the retreat.

I tell him it's for people whose parents are divorced. I don't really know much about it. Whenever they were talking about it, I wasn't paying attention. I don't tell him I'm envisioning us singing *Kumbaya* and stuff. Maybe I'll get some new perspective on life.

"What I find interesting about you guys from divorced families," he says between bites, "is you talk about it like it was so hard, but in such a casual way. I mean, is it that big a deal? It happened years ago. Can't you leave it behind and move on?"

I'm not sure what to say, so I reach for a spring roll and dipping sauce.

"People say divorce totally messes up the kids," Roger continues, "but my friends whose parents are divorced turned out great. Great education, great jobs, awesome relationships. You guys seem like a bunch of high-achievers. Is it really so bad—parents fighting to buy you stuff and take you places?" he asks with a laugh.

I don't think he's trying to offend, but, what an idiot! Really—we made up the idea that divorce is a big deal for kicks? We invented stats about school performance, addiction, poverty, depression, suicide, anxiety, self-harm, abuse, jail time, and emotional trauma for entertainment?[45]

Part of what he says is true—kids of divorce are experts at downplaying what happened. We work hard to give the impression our lives are like everyone else's. Motivated by fear of abandonment, we learn to say and be whatever people want. If we're lucky, we find a way to succeed in school or sports or the social world. Fear is a powerful motivator.

I don't say any of those things to Roger. I don't have the energy to defend myself and all the divorced children of the world—especially since he has it all figured out. Instead, I say, "I agree, Roger, us kids of divorce are a confusing bunch, trying, like the rest of the world, to make sense of this train-wreck called life.

"Would you say it's true you kids from married families are a bunch of sissies who have to live in your parents' basement eating mommy's cooking until you're thirty because you never learned to take care of yourselves? That's what it looks like to me."

With that I get up, take my plate, and go to my room to finish packing for the weekend.

***

The most serious problem with divorce happy-talk is that it lies to children. Children of divorce typically experience painful losses, moral confusion, spiritual suffering, strained or broken relationships, and higher rates of all kinds of social problems. But divorce happy-talk insists that children's experience is just the opposite.[46]

***

Friday, 9:12 pm

Sal

To: geoff.marshall@churchonthehill.com
From: spdickensfield@qtmail.com
Subject: Two good stats for you

Hi Pastor Geoff,

I hope you're well. Just about to head out for Banff—it'll probably be intense, but I think we're expecting that. Thanks for praying for us.

You told me to pass anything interesting from the retreat your way, so here are a couple quotes I found while I was preparing. I hope they'll encourage you as you plan the marriage seminar. There's nothing like heading to a retreat about divorce to make a person think about marriage.

"Research over the past decade has shown that a major share of divorces (50 to 66 percent, depending on the study) occur between couples who had average happiness and low levels of conflict in the years before the divorce."[47]

and

"Contrary to popular belief, only a minority of divorcing couples experience high conflict and abuse during their marriages. Most divorces occur with couples who have drifted apart and handle everyday disagreements poorly. It is these 'average' divorces that research shows are most harmful to children."[48]

Were you aware of those stats? I sure wasn't.

Anyway... thanks for running the marriage seminar! Please keep doing stuff like that. If the church doesn't show each generation what love and commitment look like, who will? Marriage is God's idea, and we both agree He's eager to help whomever will ask.

Have a super week,
Sal

***

COME HOME LAUGHING

Saturday, 6:30 am

Sloane

Morning people make me crazy. I climb into the backseat of Jake's car with my pillow, mumbling something about how people should have permission to sleep in on Saturdays.

Sal had wrestled the details into place for me to go to the retreat—just like she said she would. I couldn't decide if I was grateful or annoyed. I say good night to the rest of the passengers and fall asleep with my head and pillow propped against the window.

***

Saturday, 10:07 am

I jolt awake as we pull off the highway into the gas station and coffee shop. A coffee and bagel might make the world livable.

It's a Saturday morning during summer, and the gas station's packed. Kids. Dogs. License plates from around the country. Gas stops always take longer than you expect.

I'm groggy and can't decide if my mood is bad or good. Job situation: horrible. Self-esteem: in the dumps. Last night I told off my roommate's boyfriend, proving, yet again, I have almost zero control over my mouth.

What is there to be in a good mood about?

Why did I let Sal talk me into this trip?

I should be at home, looking for a job.

But getting away for the week is one way to deny the reality of my situation. I can go for a whole week forgetting my last day at work, my conversation with Roger, my bank account balance.

Can I handle so many new people in the same place at once? What kinds of bizarre things will they make me do once I'm there?

Forget about the bagel—I definitely need more sleep.

***

Saturday, 12:35 pm

The car rolls into a rest area and stops. I've been awake for the last hour, leaning on my pillow, listening to Jake and Rachel talk about their hopes for the retreat. Is it still eavesdropping when you can't not hear the conversation?

We get the cooler from the trunk and open it up on a picnic table. Rachel flew in from Vancouver last week to go to a wedding shower, is driving up with us, and will catch a ride back home after the retreat. She wanders off to take photos with her fancy camera, and Connor gets on the phone with his girlfriend.

Jake and I stretch to get rid of the I've-been-squashed-in-the-car-all-morning feeling.

"I have a confession to make," I say between bites of my cucumber sandwich.

"Oh yeah?"

"I've been awake the last hour and heard everything you and Rachel were talking about. I didn't mean to eavesdrop…"

"That's fine with me," he says. "We had a lot to catch up on, and nothing we said is secret." I think he means it.

"Is it always easy for you to talk about deep stuff?" I ask.

"Well, it's gotten normal, but it hasn't always been easy."

"No pain, no gain, is that what it is?"

"Maybe… but the good news is, you too can learn the ways of a Jedi, young Skywalker," he says. After a few bites, he continues. "Actually, it reminds me of my first year in Montreal. I'd studied French in high school and University, but I only used it for assignments or trying to look cool."

"Poser," I tease.

"Yeah, the truth comes out. I didn't realize how intense total immersion would be. I'd mix up basic words and embarrass myself on a regular basis. I went to bed exhausted every night."

"I bet you've got funny stories."

"That's for sure," he laughs. "The thing is, my brain was doing the equivalent of hundreds of mental backflips every day. It's a lot of work to make something foreign for you become natural. Gradually, so gradually I could hardly see it, I was I growing. They say kids hear over a million words before they start speaking. If that's the case, I was expecting a lot of myself in a short amount of time."

"Wow, I didn't realize it was so much work to learn another language," I comment.

"I deserve a pat on the back!" He gives himself an awkward thump on the shoulder. "Actually there are a lot of similarities between learning French and being open with people."

"*Oui*?" I ask.

"Well, just like anything you want to learn, it starts out awkward… embarrassing… uncomfortable. But the more you practice speaking from the heart, the more natural it becomes. After a while, you don't even realize you're doing it—you've simply become an open person."

"So it's a 'practice makes perfect' thing?" I ask.

"Something like that. First step, you risk being vulnerable. Then you evaluate the experience. Adjust what didn't work and give it another go," he counts off on his fingers.

"Tell yourself 'I'm not the only person who feels like this,'" I add.

"Yes. And finally, be secure, because God thinks you're fantastic!"

"Ha, ha. Yeah, I'm fantastic!" I say, matching his tone of voice.

"And, contrary to common thought—most people respect you more, not less, once they've heard your story."

Chapter Nine

Stories are so fundamental to our identity that we don't know what to do without one... I can't answer the question, "What ought I to do?" unless I have already answered a prior question, "Of which story am I a part?"[49]

Saturday, 4:48 pm

Sloane

It's mid-afternoon when we arrive at the campsite. We claim a site for us and one for Sal's carful, since they'll be coming later. The bugs are bad this early in the day, and my dark mood returns.

It doesn't take long to make camp, and all I have energy for is sitting in a lawn chair and drinking Coke. Jake and Rachel go to town for a bag of ice and a few additions to our dinner menu. Connor joins me. There must not be good cell service here, or he'd probably be on the phone with his girl. He reminds me of a friend from high school, which fools me into thinking I know him better than I do.

"I've been thinking," I begin, "wondering, actually, what's the point of all this stuff?"

"What stuff?" he asks.

"You know—driving for hours to spend an entire week talking about our family issues. Dwelling on how we've been hurt and how miserable we are. Trying to feel less hurt... so what?"

"You mean, why not just stay miserable, since life's going to pass us by anyway?"

"Yeah. That's what I mean." I slap a few mosquitos and spray more repellant on my feet and ankles. "You tell me—what do you hope to get out of

93

this retreat? Why spend your time and money and do all the weird things they're gonna make us do? What's in it for you?"

"What exactly were you drinking from that travel mug?" he asks with a smile. I shrug my shoulders and give him an innocent look. "You'll never know," I laugh.

"I'm not going to answer those exact questions," Connor says, "but I read a book about our lives as part of a story. The author gave a 250-page answer to your question: What's life about? Why do we do anything? What does it matter?"[50]

"Do you have a 250-page answer?" I ask.

"Nah. Since time is limited, I'll summarize. Life, the writer says, is supposed to be an amazing story. Well, two overlapping stories, actually."

"I'm confused already."

"Patience, my friend. Or do you have somewhere else to be?" He waves to the empty campsite and the tents.

"Go on, then."

"It was a good book, by the way. The first concept is that you, Sloane, are the main character of your life story. You have a significant say in what kind of story it's going to be. I can see it already," he pretends to film me with an imaginary camera. "Ladies and gentlemen, the amazing Sloane, making her mark on the world!"

"Oh boy. I wouldn't pay much to watch that," I answer.

"Just you wait," he says. "The second story is much bigger—it's the story of the Creator of the universe overcoming the forces of evil to bring unprecedented restoration to the world."

"That one doesn't sound so bad," I admit.

"Thought you'd like it. Anyway, if we're going to live a good story, we must understand what makes a good story."

"You're asking me?" I say when he doesn't continue.

"Do you see anyone else?"

"Sassy!" I humph. "You want to know what makes a good story?" I ask and Connor nods.

"Ok, first of all you need cool costumes... a good costume goes a long way. Killer special effects. Catchy soundtrack."

"Um-hum," Connor says, rolling his eyes.

"Fine, I can do serious. A good story is about the characters... ones you can relate to, but they should be more interesting than you are."

"Yeah, they should be likable, believable. What else?"

"There's always a problem they have to deal with—surviving the Hunger Games or defeating Prince Humperdinck."

"Problems make for interesting movies," he agrees.

"But Connor, movies are predictable. Try all you want, the characters are nothing like me. The hero always gets some superpower and saves the world in two hours. Meanwhile, my life goes on as normal. Movies are made up." This conversation is not answering my questions.

"Yeah, yeah, I hear you—it's Hollywood. But there's something to learn from how the characters respond to challenges. The bigger the challenge, the better the story. The more risk, the more you care what happens. Think about Katniss and Westley at the beginning and then at the end of their stories. What happened? What shaped them?"

"Fine," I grumble. They are some of my favorites. "Katniss was the underdog. She risked her life for her sister. She faced her fears. She made some friends. Westley fell in love with the beautiful maiden, got kidnapped by a pirate, learned to swordfight, didn't give up hope. He found Buttercup, got betrayed again, overcame the bad guy, and finally got the girl back."

"Good memory. I love those movies!" Connor laughs. "Different storylines, different heroes, but similar progression. They found themselves in a crappy situation, faced their fears, took risks, made friends, experienced joy. Take away the details, and it sounds a bit like my life."

"Shall I call you 'Dread Pirate Connor'?" I must admit, the guy is likable.

"As you wish, Cupcake," he says, rising to his feet and brandishing an imaginary sword. He sits down again. "I'm not sure what your life's been like, but what if we looked at our lives as if they were part of a movie? Our happy, normal life got messed up. Now we're trying to figure out how to make it better. The question is—what kind of characters will we be?"

"I'd probably die the first day of the Hunger Games."

"Stop being so positive!" Connor scolds. "What if this is the part of our story where transformation happens? What if we can make friends, discover inner strength, face our fears? Every good story involves struggle and failure and some discouragement. Nobody wants that, but it's where the real action is."

"So you want to know what kind of movie they'd make of my life?" I ask. It's an interesting thought.

"That's one way to think about it," he says. "If that's the case, I must be in the character development part of my story." He pauses and drinks some Coke. "I hope I'm headed in the right direction. These days, I feel I'm in a dark tunnel. I can't see much light, but I keep moving anyway."

"Is that the same as going through the motions?" I ask. "What if you're going the wrong direction? How will you know?"

"Going through the motions implies purposelessness. I'm not sitting on the couch watching Netflix all day. I'm not exactly sure where I'm going, but I'm pointing myself toward God. I'm trying to be intentional with my choices. And I've been taking notes from the way Sal and Jake live. Hopefully I've learned something from them."

"It makes sense... to look at my life as a movie, a novel. But to be honest, it's a pretty pathetic story so far." If he can be honest, so can I.

"I hear ya. Tell me, if you don't mind, what part of your story is so pathetic?" he asks.

"Well..." I sit up a bit straighter and clear my throat. "The main character is a dud: unemployed and single. Her life got messed up as a kid, and she's been stuck since. Not much to report, apart from running some 10Ks. She doesn't fight bad guys or save her little sister. She wouldn't recognize true love if it knocked her on the head... but there's no danger of that." It was even more pathetic out loud. Did my voice crack?

"Sloane, Sloane. I don't know enough about your life to agree or disagree, and it doesn't matter what I think. Truth is, you were created for a purpose, and you can live a really a good story."

I'm not sure what to do at this point. Boiling it down like that is brutal. I thought my day couldn't get any worse, but I was wrong. I hate being stuck here without a car. I stand up to walk away.

"Sloane, wait a minute." Connor reaches up and takes my arm. "Please, sit back down. There's more."

His voice is kind. I sit back down.

"I said we're part of two stories, remember?"

I nod.

"There's the story of Sloane. The story of Connor," he says quietly. "Then there's the story of God."

"Are you gonna quote Bible verses?" I ask. I imagine Sunday School colouring books and Veggie Tales. Children's stories don't help anymore.

"I do enjoying quoting the Bible, when helpful, but I think I can cover this one without getting preachy," he says gently.

I nod again. Let's see where he goes.

"In God's story, He's the focus of attention. Not because He has to be told how great He is, since He already knows, but because He dreamed it up. He's the One who makes it happen. He's the only character in the story from start to finish. He's the One with the most at stake. The camera stays focused on Him, because that's where the action happens. There are other characters with significant parts, but the story exists because of God. Take God out of the story, and there's no story.

"Some people hear this and conclude they're too small to matter, but that's not the case. The difference in size between us and Him doesn't stop God from caring about us. When we recognize the story is about Him, we get the right perspective on life and the universe. Our lives are short. There is so much we just don't get. God sees the big picture, and He has the long view.

"It's through Him we get in on the story. We are connected to Him and part of His amazing forever. We're not stuck on the outside trying to figure out how to get included—we're on the inside. And what this does is call us to think bigger. If all we see is the here and now, we make lame decisions. We're important, but we aren't the only ones who are important.

"We didn't get here on our own. People like Sal and Pastor Geoff and Jake helped us. We've been given a lot. What we do with this life can impact generations to come. God has given me a voice in His story, and I don't want to waste it."

"Connor, a big, important life sounds cool, and some people have that, but if life is such a great story, why does mine totally suck?" I ask. I don't want to rain on his parade, but it sounds completely random to me— and unfair. "Why do so many people live pointless, painful lives? What about that?" Idealism has some merit, but the guy needs a reality check.

"I don't want to sound trite, because pain in a bad story is legit, but maybe those people are living the wrong story," he says. "They don't know what they're made for. They don't see the big picture. They feel expendable."

"But it's not fair to say people who have crappy lives just can't think of anything better," I counter. "Lots of people didn't choose the crap that happened to them. They are actual victims of bad stuff."

"I agree with that. Living a meaningful life takes more than a positive attitude and some pom-poms. Question is, does bad stuff have to be the final word? Think about Katniss."

"Clearly she got screwed over," I say. "Twice."

"Yeah, she did. But the story didn't end there. Why not?" he asks.

"She had something to live for... a goal that kept her from giving up. She wanted to protect her sister, to see her again. Eventually some people came along to help her. She worked hard." Katniss is so cool.

"And Westley?" Connor asks. "He was kidnapped, forced into slavery..."

"True. That's the non-fairy tale part of the story. I haven't thought much about those five years he was stuck on a pirate ship. Somehow he lived through each day without giving up."

"And he learned how to be a completely awesome pirate while he was at it!" Connor's eyes widen at the thought.

"Connor," I say, "it seems easy for people to get their lives together in the movies, but it hasn't worked the same in my life. You can't just order someone to show up in your life and help you out."

"That's true," he pauses. "But have they?"

"Have they what?"

"Have any people shown up in your life to help you out?"

"Oh." I hadn't thought of it that way. I consider Sal, Pastor Geoff, Chloe. "Yeah," I say, "they have. But things keep getting worse in my life, not better, even with help."

"You're here, aren't you? On your way to a retreat to sort out your life."

"Is that what I'm going to do this week?" I laugh sarcastically. "The only reason I'm here is I got fired."

"Oh, I didn't know that part," he replies. "Not to one-up you, but the only reason I'm here is I can't have healthy relationships. I'm twenty-seven, almost finished my Master's, but I still don't know who I am or what I want from life. Seems to me you're in a pretty good place."

"Are you making fun of me?" I ask.

"Nah, not at all. I'm saying you're in a time of life where change can happen. In the movies, there's always a moment of decision. Maybe you're in that moment now. You're going to the retreat, which is a good sign. Friends have appeared, and they like you.

You aren't running any more... Sounds promising to me."

"Yeah, maybe," I agree. "And who cares if I've been clueless until now! So what if we've lived as faceless extras, confused about the story we are supposed to live!"

Connor stands up. "So what if our hope is fragile and anemic?" he shouts. He takes a Superman pose and declares, "Things are about to change!"

We high-five, and he sits down again. "You got fired. My relationships stink. These are mere plot twists, Sloane. One day we'll look back and see how far we've come." This guy is miles ahead of me.

"I hope you're right, Connor."

"Me too," he says sheepishly. "But even if I'm not, God has great things in store for us. If we look to Him, we can't go wrong."

I smile in reply, "Thanks for the chat." My head is about to explode.

"You're welcome," he says.

"I think it's time for a walk." If only I could make it back home. "I won't go far."

***

We long for spirituality as much as our peers from intact families do, but loss, sufferings, lack of trust in and anger at our parents, and even anger at God are more defining qualities of our spiritual journeys.[51]

From the viewpoint of the children, and counter to what happens to their parents, divorce is a cumulative experience. Its impact increases over time and rises to a crescendo in adulthood. At each developmental stage, divorce is experienced anew in different ways. In adulthood it affects personality, the ability to trust, expectations about relationships, and ability to cope with change.[52]

Chapter Ten

Sunday, 5:48 pm

Sloane

We had planned to arrive by three, but of course there was construction. We'd inched along the mountain roads. I didn't complain—honestly, I wasn't in a hurry to get here. When we were still on the road, no one could make me do anything I didn't want.

The retreat centre is way nicer than expected. I'm sharing a room with Rachel, who drove up with me. We don't start until seven, which means there's time for a run and shower before we start.

I forget how hard it is to run at altitude. I get out of the shower at 6:40 and scramble to get ready on time. So much for making a good impression. My hair is wet, and my face is still red. I have a feeling I'm going to look much worse by the end of the week.

***

Saturday, 7:02 pm

A woman named Katherine meets us in the lobby. She has a nice smile and dark hair streaked with white. She hands each of us a nametag without hesitation, though she's never met us before. Impressive. There are eight of us from Saskatoon, six from Vancouver, and four from Edmonton.

We walk outside to a stone patio overlooking the Bow River. White Christmas lights, citronella candles, vases of flowers, background music, and patio furniture with cushions give it the feel of an outdoor living room.

There's a table of food. My stomach growls.

We mingle around the food, and I meet almost everyone by the time Katherine asks us to sit.

"Welcome again. It's a pleasure to have this week with you," she begins. "There are many places you could be this week instead of here, and you all have made sacrifices to attend this retreat. I am honoured to be part of this gathering, and we have been carefully planning our time together.

"This group is diverse in many ways, but all of you are from a divorced family. Divorce has shaped your lives in a number of ways. Many people downplay the impact of divorce, but we won't. You have come with a desire for change, and this is key to what we will explore this week. This week will not be easy because change is not easy.

"It's normal to run from pain, but pain is a gift. Pain draws attention to what is important. Pain keeps you alive. But what often happens is we ignore pain and eventually lose the ability to feel much at all. The pain goes numb, but so does the joy and hope and warmth you long for. Your self-protection skills keep you from the life you want.

"You have come seeking healing and restoration," she continues, "and I believe you can learn and change. The kind of change you need will require you to alter your ways of thinking, feeling, and relating. Each of you have a wonderful, God-given capacity to grow and change. He is with you in this. He understands what it is to be human. He wants to help you.

"You might wonder what qualifies me to lead you. I am not from a divorced family, nor am I divorced myself. I was married, for almost a year, to a lovely man named Vinny. One afternoon, while I was happily working at the bookstore, he was murdered. I have been a widow for over twenty years now. I mention this as a way to say that I am acquainted with loss and pain. I spent years ignoring my anger and hurt, then years learning to understand them. I have searched for and found great joy along the way.

"I am trained as a counselor and spiritual director. Our team has been praying for you. We are here to answer questions, to pray, to talk, and to assist in whatever way we can.

"I'm deeply sorry for what you have been through. Your pain matters to God. Your past does not need to be the final word for you.

"Our team has chosen a Scripture verse for each of you, and you will find it written on a card in your room. Tonight's homework is to write a journal entry in response to that verse.

"Sleep well, and I look forward to being together again in the morning. Oh… and unless you'd like some creaturely visits during the night, I suggest you close your balcony doors."

***

Saturday, 9:23 pm

Sloane's Journal

My verse is Isaiah 49:15-16:

Can a woman forget her nursing child,
And have no compassion on the son of her womb?
Even these may forget,
but I will not forget you.
Behold, I have inscribed you on the palms of My hands;
Your walls are continually before Me.

I pull my journal to me and start writing.

Rejection is nothing new. Mothers have been rejecting their own children since Bible times. Well, at least I'm not alone. It's ridiculous, though—it goes against everything motherhood is "supposed" to be about.

I wonder what happened to kids back then who didn't have a mom. Who took care of them? At least these days, Children's Services will find someone to keep you.

God says, "When no one is there to care for you, I will care for you. You are important to Me. I notice you. I will show you the love and compassion your mother never did."

It sucks to be forgotten. My life reads like the Forgotten Child textbook... left behind at school. Forgotten birthdays. Waiting at the door with a bag packed for trips that never happened.

Flesh and blood meant nothing to the woman who carried me in her womb.

Lord, how does Your promise change anything for me?

The image of God writing my name on His palm sounds funny to me. Is it a tattoo? Is He writing with a Bic pen?

If it's a tattoo, that's pretty cool. No matter where He goes, that tattoo goes with Him. Tattoos last longer than emotions and outlast disagreements. They endure offenses and jealousy.

I like the idea of God choosing me and not going back on His choice.

I haven't thought much about being chosen by Him. Does He love me because He wants to, or because He's God and loves everyone? If He's not "obligated" to love me but chooses to do so, that's quite impressive.

Each moment, every day, He wants me. He remembers me. He sees my name written on His hand, and He smiles as He thinks of me.

I have some friends with babies, and I can picture the way they hold and cuddle their babies. What would it feel like to have God be that attentive and compassionate toward me?

I wish I could turn back the clock and go through my childhood with God as my Mom.

***

Saturday, 9:48 pm

Rachel's Journal

For you have been bought with a price: therefore glorify God in your body.
1 Corinthians 6:20

Seriously! I get the verse that talks about what to do with your body? Not funny.

Where are the verses about forgiveness and treasures in heaven and stuff like that? That's the verses I want—not a spotlight on everything I feel bad about.

Why does God care so much about my body? My spirit is what matters, right? I'm just passing time here until I die. Why worry about the earthly stuff?

Yes, I did stupid things with my body. It was a way to piss off my parents. My body was the one thing I had control over. I dressed it how I wanted and shared it with whomever I wanted. Mom hardly noticed. Dad might have noticed but never said so.

Did they even care about me, or was my body another thing to fight over? Who controls Rachel now? I was just a pawn to them.

Back to the verse…

I have to say, it doesn't have the same feel of control about it. God cares about my body because He cares about me. He thinks I'm valuable. You don't throw something valuable on the floor. You take care of it. You pay attention to it.

God says my body (I) can be used for good. My body (I) can glorify God…?? Whatever that means.

When I read "glory," I think of things that are shiny, beautiful, glowing.

Could my body (I) shine for God?

Is that what having a body is about—a physical way of showing God's brightness here and now? Dunno.

The choice is mine. I can decide how to use the body (life) He's given me. He doesn't *force* me to live in a certain way.

Mom and Dad acted like they owned me… two toddlers fighting over a toy. But God's not rubbing in how much I owe Him. He's not making demands. Instead, He's asking, and I can almost hear a "please."

"Rachel, please glorify Me with your body."

The choice is mine. No manipulation.

"I give this body to you, and I trust you with it."

Lord, I have mistreated the body You gave me. I've made stupid decisions with it, and I let others mistreat it. I'm sorry I didn't see myself or my body the way You do.

If You're still willing to let me, I'd like to shine for You.

Chapter Eleven

Our longing for belonging is an innate and undeniable part of our makeup... Our fears of being dismissed, let down, betrayed, abandoned, or rejected stifle our willingness to risk authenticity and vulnerability as an adult. We send mixed "Come here!/Go away!" signals.[53]

One of the most important aspects to growth in our suffering is that we need to know that we are understood. This is what empathy provides for us. We cannot grow if we are all alone emotionally. Life is too difficult.[54]

Monday, 8:56 am

Sloane

Day One: Created to Belong

I never sleep well in a strange bed, which explains a lot about my sleep-deprived childhood.

Breakfast at the retreat is self-serve, come-when-you're-ready: the way I like it. People talk about the weather and the best coffee shops from home. It reminds me of the first day of university—everyone on good behavior, eager to impress, kind of awkward, unsure what to expect.

We get to the meeting room before nine. I'd imagined a doctor's office, sterile and cold, where we'd sit and dissect our lives. We'd open up old, festering wounds, try to clean out infections that never kill us but never manage to heal.

Instead… matching couches. Pillows and throw blankets. Natural light. Fresh flowers. It feels more like the first day at an expensive rehab centre. I laugh to myself. Perhaps that's exactly what this is.

Knowing everyone is a child of divorce is a relief. Comfort in shared misery. I don't have to defend myself from the "attack of the perfect family" feeling that creeps up around intact (non-divorced) families. It's a mixture of jealousy, anger, sadness, and the sensation that I don't measure up. It doesn't matter what I'm wearing, how much I know, how successful or popular I am; I become acutely aware that I'm flawed beyond repair. It's a bitter taste I can't get rid of, and it spoils everything.

I find a seat in a comfortable-looking armchair near the back and notice the verses on the whiteboard:

Long before he laid down earth's foundations, he has us in mind, had settled on us as the focus of his love, to be made whole and holy by his love. Long, long ago he decided to adopt us into his family through Jesus Christ. (What pleasure he took in planning this!)[55]
Ephesians 1:4-6

Katherine waits for us to find seats and then begins. "I had a great aunt who often said, 'What you want and what you get ain't often the same.' It was her way of saying, 'Stop your whining,' but she never explained why life was unfair. Even as a little kid, it bothered me that I couldn't get what I wanted. Why was life so difficult? I never asked her those things, of course. You didn't question Great-Aunt Irene.

"Her saying revealed a universal truth: Life is no longer what it should be. Something has gone wrong. What we see on earth is different from what God intended. People's choices cause damage. Sometimes we get hurt, and sometimes we cause the hurt.

"We find ourselves in situations we didn't choose. We experience fear. We become hard and bitter. We lash out. We self-destruct. How are we to respond when we find ourselves in a situation that never should have been?

"Let's move from the general to the individual. Each of you experienced the divorce of your parents, the break-up of your family of origin. Regardless of how necessary it may have been, how well it was explained, or how it affected you, I propose that divorce in and of itself is not what God intended for you. It's not what He intended for any child.

"God is a relationship expert. He can teach you what you didn't learn from your first family. He has included you in a family radically different from what you have known—a relationship perfect in love and generosity, one built on a solid foundation. Among the Trinity, commitment and consistency have been in operation for eternity.[56]

"You said 'Yes!' to joining this family. Though none of us understand exactly what it means, you are discovering how to be God's son or daughter.

"You have already experienced healing in some areas. However, there are emotions, thoughts, and perceptions that need additional work. As followers of Jesus, we live in an 'in-between' time. Christ has defeated the enemy and established God's kingdom, but we do not yet see its fulfillment.[57]

"The apostle John said it like this: 'Beloved, now we are children of God, and it has not appeared as yet what we will be.'[58] We are His children, but there is still some working out to do. This in-between time is a painful place to be, a place of waiting, but it is hopeful as well. We are stumbling along, looking through a dark glass, trying to see God as He is, trying to understand who we are, trying to let His love change us.[59]

"This week we will talk about divorce. We will discuss human development, attachment, emotional maturity, grief, and loss. We will talk about hope and restoration. We will explore the role of community in growth and healing. You will share your story with others.

"But before we get to that, we must, *must* root ourselves in an awareness that we belong to God. It is in Christ we find out who we are and what we are living for.[60]

"There are many philosophies and therapies out there. You may have tried some. I've tried most of them. I discovered that any system without God at the foundation cannot bring freedom or hope.

"This understanding will not come as a one-click-download-and-install. It's another example of the 'already but not yet.' I know I'm His, but I don't completely know what that means yet. I have experienced restoration, but everything has not been sorted out yet."

Katherine pauses, walks to the whiteboard, and puts up a quote:

> People's most basic need in life is relationship. People connected to other people thrive and grow, and those not connected wither and die. It is a medical fact, for example, that from infancy to old age, health depends on the amount of social connection people have.[61]

"You were created for relationship and inclusion. I'm not saying the goal is to be cool or popular, but to be *known*. Your experience may have communicated that you were unwanted, rejected, and forgotten—by people who were supposed to love you. You were never supposed to live without love and acceptance. As a fish thrives in water, you thrive when you are surrounded by love.[62]

"You can comprehend God's love on an intellectual level but exist for years without experiencing this love. You may not even realize there is more."

For a while, I'm so full of what Katherine has said that I can't take in any more. I tune out to mull it over. When I finally tune back in, Katherine is telling a story about a girl named Jenny who lived with her parents in a cottage in the woods. When enemy soldiers approach her house, Jenny's mom tells her to run and hide in the woods until it's safe to return.[63]

The soldiers capture Jenny's parents and chase after her. To stay safe, Jenny stays hidden in the woods. She sees danger in every noise and shadow. She never lets her guard down.

The war ends and the country is safe again, but Jenny doesn't know. From her perspective, nothing has changed. She lives as a fugitive, afraid for her life. She runs from everyone, even those trying to tell her the war is over. Sadly, the skills that protected her in a time of danger now keep her alone and in fear.

What hope is there for Jenny?

Katherine asks us to consider how we might be like Jenny. What does hiding look like in our lives? Do we realize it's safe to come out of the woods?

We all agree Jenny is in a bad situation. What kept her alive in the past now keeps her isolated and afraid.

***

> When a legitimate, God-given need goes
> unmet because of neglect or attack, that part
> of us goes into shock, just as we do when we're
> injured in a car accident. It begins to
> withdraw...The longer and deeper the
> isolation, the greater the injury...[64]

***

Monday, 11:00 am

> When we hide, a part of our character is
> pushed away from relationships into a spiritual
> darkness called isolation. The isolation of some
> part of our soul from love will always produce
> a problem... In the physical world we call this
> malnutrition. Spiritual and emotional
> malnutrition are just as destructive...[65]

***

David, a fifty-something member of the team, leads the next session. He talks about how experience shapes our understanding of the world. We often claim our decisions and choices are based on logic, values, and beliefs. But what we say we believe and what we choose to do are often quite different. There's a disconnect.

He suggests there is another, deeper layer at work in us. We have absorbed an understanding of the world through our experience. We have been shaped at a subconscious level, to some degree, by the story we believe we are a part of.

He asks a lot of questions to make us think: In what areas do our words and actions not line up? We can say we are loved, but do we act like it? We say God cares for us, but do we live relaxed and carefree lives?

Perhaps our emotions and beliefs and decision-making abilities are more complex and intertwined than we realize.

Information does not automatically transform us. Information is important, but change requires more than information. For example, we say God loves us, but many of us struggle to feel accepted and loved. So which is more accurate—that we believe we are loved, or that we don't believe it? Information and experience must go together. Otherwise we live an inconsistent, roller-coaster kind of life. It reminds me of what Sal told me about emotional memory.

I have the feeling that half of everything that happens this week will go over my head. I don't hate smart people, but I like *wikipedia*. I wonder what keywords I ought to search.

As he keeps talking, the dots start to connect for me.

Truth: God loves us.

Truth: God is close to us.

We agree those statements are true. However, if we can't recognize what love or closeness or trust feel like, we continue to live as though we are unloved and alone.

David uses the analogy of radio waves. You could read books about radio waves and talk about how amazing they are, but until a radio is switched on and tuned to a specific frequency, you cannot decipher the message the waves are carrying.

Children of divorce often identify feelings of loneliness and insecurity. Fear of rejection and abandonment are unconscious factors in our decisions. Before we can change, we need to recognize what's going on. We have to learn to tune in to experiences of love and connection. We have to take risks of being vulnerable and authentic.

***

If, as theologian Bernard Cooke writes, 'it is primarily in loving and being loved that we begin to grasp the incredible truth that we are loved by God,' what happens to children's faith when someone they love has left?[66]

***

David tells us that he used to make it a habit to be the first person to leave any gathering. He didn't notice this pattern until a friend commented on it. David realized it was his fear of being left behind which motivated him to leave first. His friend challenged him to try an experiment—be the last one to leave every event for an entire week. Was his fear of being left behind a reality, or a ghost from his past? It was an experiment in vulnerability.

For our next activity, we have to tell a story about a time we experienced relational closeness with a friend, family member, or stranger. "Non-sexual closeness, that is!" David clarifies, grinning. We laugh.

I remember spending the weekend with a family who went to our church while the husband was working on his PhD. Heather and I met at a work-bee when we were assigned window-washing duty together. We bonded during the hours of ladders and Windex. Heather was hilarious, and I laughed so much my stomach hurt. After that, Heather was intentional in finding me each week after the service and asking how I was doing, even while corralling her rambunctious kids.

Our schedules were complicated, but Heather looked for ways to include me in her life. She'd call on the fly, inviting me to a cartoon matinee, a trip to the park, ice-skating, soccer games. Conversations were always interrupted, but I liked being part of their family.

One time she asked me to spend the night: Friday dinner, popcorn and a movie, Saturday-morning pancakes. I felt comfortable enough to accept. The three kids required a lot of attention from Mom and Dad, so I had to entertain myself, which was fine with me.

I got up early on Saturday and sipped my coffee on the deck overlooking a lake. Before long, seven-year-old Sarah joined me outside. She was in her PJs, with dramatic bedhead, carrying her blankie. Still sleepy, she snuggled with me, wanting to be near. I wasn't used to having anyone so close to me for so long. It was nice, but odd. When Heather called us to breakfast, I was reluctant to move.

As I share my story with the other people in my retreat group, I treasure the memory of watching the steam rise from my coffee and soaking up the view with little Sarah. Sitting together on the porch had no practical purpose, and it didn't change the world, but it was nice to feel close and connected and happy.

***

If you allow yourself to be known by God, you invite a different and frankly more terrifying experience. You are now in a position of vulnerability. If you permit others to know you, they can make their own assessment of your worth... You grant them the option to love you or to reject you. In essence, you must—must—trust another with yourself.[67]

117

Monday, 2:00 pm

When we return from lunch, the room has been rearranged. Chairs are clustered in threes, and there are name cards on each seat.

We find our places, and Katherine begins.

"This week we will consider who you are in light of who God is. He created you, in love, for a purpose. You have been shaped by your past, and some of what you experienced is very different from what God intended for you. As you consider the events of your childhood, ask God to help you see how your parents' divorce or divorces have shaped you.

"Before we start the next activity, I'll explain our two guidelines. The first is that everyone listens when someone is talking. When I say 'listen,' I mean no interrupting, no correcting, and... wait for it... *no advice*.

"Second, after you talk, let two others speak before you talk again. This will include the introverts and extroverts in the conversation." As she speaks, she walks through the room, making eye contact with each of us.

"Let me warn you—talking about your past will stir emotions and push your buttons like nothing else. Remember, though, everyone in this room is on your side."

We nod in response.

"Our next activity is the telling of your narrative. Each of you will have thirty minutes to tell your story to the others in your triplet. Many adult children of divorce have never shared their entire story with anyone. I know you will listen well.

"Before you start talking, I'll give you time to sketch a timeline or outline of your life, focusing on your parents' divorce and your childhood. I'll list some categories you can use as a framework."

On the board, she writes:

- Events
- People
- Relationships
- Emotions
- Losses
- Conflict
- Memories—good and bad

We write in silence until Katherine says to stop. Then we begin telling our stories to each other. Thirty minutes sounded like a long time, but it turns out we have a lot to say. If Katherine didn't kept us on track, we could have gone on for hours.

The people in my group are amazing. Truly.

Their stories are so sad. The disappointments of little children make me angry. I picture them as kids walking through a field of snakes and landmines. How did they become such strong, mature adults? How did they survive such loss and injustice? They didn't deserve what happened to them.

When it's my turn (I wait until the end, of course), I'm amazed that the words keep coming out of my mouth. I'm never as candid with strangers as I am with these two.

I don't cry, but the two in my group are the ones shedding tears as I describe the first days after Mom left. I talk about feeling invisible, the abuse, my life at home after the divorce. I've never had strangers cry about my life before. I don't even cry about it. I keep telling them it's not a big deal and they don't have to be so upset, but the tears don't stop.

How can I wrap up a conversation like this, especially since the story is still unfolding? I can't say, "It's all finished and behind me now." Memories I

119

haven't thought of in years come back to mind, vivid and pungent. My words trickle off, and we sit in silence. I feel relief when it's over, the way my feet feel when I take off my ice skates—relieved, tired, sore, but oh, so good.

***

> One of the aspects of genuine, healthy relatedness is that people don't hide their vulnerability from one another and are not ashamed of who they are before each other.[68]

Chapter Twelve

Monday, 4:20 pm

Sloane

We've moved to the patio during break to soak in the sunshine, and Katherine joins us with her tea in hand to debrief. She explains how important it is to pay attention to what's going on inside us during an activity. The inner process is as valuable as the activity itself.

"What was it like to be the speaker?" she asks.

"It was harder than I thought to tell the story from start to finish," a woman named Kimmie says. "In my mind, it's like a ball of yarn—tangled and messy. As I talked, I saw how the events and people and things I've struggled with are connected, which was cool."

Connor adds, "I'd never thought about those categories you wrote on the board. I'd never made a list of the losses in my life, and it got scary long. People always told me to be thankful for what I had, but no one discussed what I didn't have. I tried to ignore what I'd missed. This gives me lots to think about."

"It was great to talk with people who understand what I've been through," Rachel says. "I didn't have to explain or leave out the shocking details. It felt good to get the dark family secrets off my chest. I feel lighter."

A young man named Manuel says, "I've spent my life protecting Mom and Dad and find it hard to be open with people. I'm not even sure what really happened and what I just imagined. I feel quite confused at the moment."

"Thank you all for your honesty," Katherine says. "These insights are worth further thought. I hope you will continue thinking about what's been said. Now, I'd like to hear what it was like to be the listener."

"I felt so honoured," Jake begins. He's standing with his arms over the shoulders of his groupmates. "I was so touched to be trusted with really deep stuff in the lives of my group. I love these two!"

"The stories in my group were really sad," Brad says softly. "Jason and Sal lived through some bad stuff. I really wish it had never happened to them!"

"I have seriously cool people in my group!" Sal says with a nod to Brad and Jason. "Their childhoods were messed up, but here they are, hanging out with me in Banff, trying to be better men instead of plotting multiple homicide. I really respect you guys for the choices you've made!"

"I didn't enjoy telling my story," Kimmie comments, "but it was totally different listening to these two... it was good to hear them talk, to be able to understand more." She pauses, then wonders out loud, "I don't know why it's like that."

Katherine has been nodding as each person speaks. When we've all fallen silent, she says, "Thank you again for sharing your experience, and for being wonderful listeners. Listening is a powerful act of love. Isn't it fascinating how a few hours of intentional connecting can bond us as a group? Can you believe it's only Monday?" We laugh at that.

"Instead of a round of applause, we'll have a round of hugs. Stand up, find someone you want to encourage, and give them a hug, or a high-five. Whichever you prefer." Soon the patio is buzzing with hugs and high-fives and smiles and more tears.

For once, I feel I'm in a group where I belong. These people understand something about me, and they aren't pushing me away. I look over at Sal and remember the Mother's Day we first talked. The way I feel at this moment is so different from how I felt then. Where would I be if I'd never met that crazy lady?

***

> Except for those raised in divorced families, few people realized the many ways that divorce shapes not only the child's life but also the child.[69]

***

The final assignment before dinner is a Scripture reflection. With fresh coffee and snacks, we each find a comfy spot to journal.

***

Jason's Reflection

And the LORD, He is the one who goes before you. He will be with you; He will not leave you nor forsake you; do not fear nor be dismayed.
Deuteronomy 31:8

Feel-good, empty promises. Does not make sense! God goes *ahead* of me and is supposed to be *with* me at the same time? Illogical. People are so quick to make promises they can't keep—like when they say, "Everything's going to be OK." Things are not always going to be OK. I'm not an idiot. People promise stuff way beyond their power to control.

- You'll find a great job; I'm sure of it!
- Of course you'll get the promotion. The boss would be crazy not to pick you!

123

- You're definitely going to get accepted to that program.
- And my personal favorite: You'll find your perfect girl *any day* now.

How can people lie with a straight face? You can't make something happen just by saying it over and over again.

Back to the verse… Moses is giving Joshua a pep talk. God's not going to leave him alone to lead Israel. Makes sense—they're God's people, after all.

Can I apply this concept to my life? Does God promise to be with me in the same way? What can I expect from Him? Why should God bother helping me? I'm not carrying the fate of a nation in my hands like Joshua.

How long before He gets tired of how much help I need?

"Do not fear or be dismayed."

How do I NOT fear? I can't just decide stuff like that.

Fear is my constant companion—an angry dog sleeping with a chain around its neck. It looks peaceful from far away, but it always wakes up barking.

What do Moses and Joshua know that I don't know?

***

Jenn's Reflection

The LORD appeared to him from afar, saying, "I have loved you with an everlasting love; therefore I have drawn you with lovingkindness."
Jeremiah 31:3

124

I dream of a guy who would follow me around the world or knock on my front door to declare his love for me. My desire for attention doesn't go away.

No guy's done that. No one's thought I was worthy of that much effort, but God pursued me.

From everlasting, HE has loved me.

From afar, HE had His eye on me.

HE's never forgotten me.

I've never been invisible to HIM.

It's hard to separate this truth from my experience with people. God seemed so far away when I was growing up. He was in church but nowhere else. Only the pastor's prayers got His attention. God was like a statue frozen in wrath. It was better to keep a healthy distance between Him and me.

The only time of year I felt close to God was Christmas. I felt different about baby Jesus. Instead of an angry face, Jesus smiled at everyone. For a few weeks each year, I wasn't scared of God.

When Mom and Dad split, we stopped going to church. Mom hated people staring at us when we went without Dad. I was happy to stay home and watch TV in my pajamas.

Everlasting love seems impossible to understand. What am I supposed to compare it to? Dad left us. Mom was stuck with us. Dad said, "I love you, and I'll see you soon," but he really meant, "I'll visit next time I feel guilty."

I never get the love I want.

What does God's extravagant love feel like? How do I get ready for the day He packs up and gives His attention to someone else?

***

Connor's Reflection

Just as I have been with Moses, I will be with you; I will not fail you or forsake you.
Joshua 1:5

Moses was a decent guy. Sure, he murdered someone, but we all make mistakes. He straightened up and wrote five books of the Bible.

Joshua was a good man, too: military commander, Moses's right-hand man. He had lots to offer.

But me—I'm a different case. Not sure anyone can stick with me.

How many of Mom's boyfriends said, "See you next week, Buddy," or "I'll take you fishing," and then disappeared? Some only stuck around long enough to find Mom's bedroom.

Joshua was lucky to have forty years with Moses. They really must have trusted each other. I don't know anybody that well. My friendships don't last. Can't get them to stick.

Joshua saw miracles first-hand. He watched the Red Sea part. He ate manna. He followed a pillar of fire through the desert. If I'd seen that kind of stuff, I'm sure I'd be a different man.

I'd like to think God will never leave me.

I've learned, though, that people are usually extra nice right before they bail. I'd prefer them to be mean instead; that way I'd feel happy after they'd left.

***

Sal's Reflection

And Jesus went up to the mountain and summoned those whom He Himself wanted, and they came to Him. And He appointed twelve, that they might be with Him...
Mark 3:13-14

Jesus chose twelve disciples, and the first thing listed in their job description was: *Be WITH Jesus.*

Be with Jesus. How come I never noticed this?

The story lists them by name. They weren't generic disciples—they were friends of Jesus. These were the guys he wanted to hang out with. Men he'd grown to trust. He picked them. He wanted them.

I don't really feel that way. I feel more replaceable than wanted.

Sure, I do a good job as a Follower—I make coffee at church and try to be friendly. I host a support group at my house, and it helps people. But I wonder what would happen if I didn't do such a good job at everything. Would He look for someone else to fill my role?

Is being with me actually important to Him?

Chapter Thirteen

Monday, 7:22 pm

Sloane

What do you do after a day like today? If I were at home, I'd go for a run or get in the car and see where it carries me. Take a nap. Clean something.

But away from home, it's difficult. There's nowhere to go.

I don't have to think about it for long, because as soon as we finish eating, Amy walks in with her purse over her shoulder. "We're going on a field trip!" she announces. "Take your plates to the kitchen and meet me in the parking lot in ten minutes. Oh... bring the formal shoes we told you about."

I like a little mystery in my life.

Rachel and I hurry to our room. I dig through my suitcase for the shoes I'd brought. I comb my hair and check my makeup. "Where would we go at this time of day with dress shoes?" I wonder to Rachel.

"I hope it involves a hot air balloon," she jokes back.

David and Evan take the guys in one van, and the ladies go with Amy. It's twenty minutes from the retreat centre to town. There are tourists with cameras and ice cream cones everywhere.

Amy parks the van in a reserved spot, leads us down an alley, up a flight of stairs, and pushes open a shop door with a large "Closed" sign in the window. We file in, and she locks the door behind us with a flourish. She's *enjoying* this.

"Ladies, you can take off your street shoes and leave them over there." She points to a shoe rack and disappears into the store, leaving us to follow orders.

By the time our shoes are off, she's back with Isabel, an older lady with glasses on a chain and a tape measure around her neck.

"Welcome to my shop, ladies," she says with a smile. "I'm glad you're here. You will be attending two special events this week, and we're here to make sure you look fabulous. Each of you must pick two outfits—one serious and one fun. Choose anything you like. If it doesn't fit off the rack, we'll make it fit. Changing rooms are there. Let's get to work."

"You heard Isabel correctly," Amy says, noticing our confusion. "You need two outfits for the week. Pick what you like, and Isabel's team will tailor items for you. Help each other out."

Lights and music come on, and it's not long before the dressing rooms are full of clothes and women and laughter. I'm not a big shopper, but it doesn't matter. Outfits are chosen by group approval. I'm not used to so many opinions about what I wear, or so many compliments. A small army of tailors appears to pin hems and waistbands.

Before long, the dresses are labeled with our names and hanging on racks at the back. We gather our purses and shoes and hug Isabel goodbye. Her assistant hands us cups of hot chocolate "for the road," and Amy leads us back to the van.

I swear there must have been something in that hot chocolate, because by the time we get back we're practically passed out. Amy doesn't give any hints about the special events, but it's a fun way to end Day One.

What are the chances I can survive four more days of this?

***

Monday, 7:35 pm

Manuel

David and Evan are waiting in the van when we get to the parking lot. Our destination for the evening is a hike to their favorite lookout. Evan hands out headlamps, since it will be dark when we come back down. Hiking by headlamp... very cool. We make a pit stop at the tailor's on the way to get measured for suits. I don't ask.

I've never been to the Rockies before. Everything is gigantic. Huge chunks of rock. Trees growing out of cliffs. It concerns me. Are they sure there's enough oxygen where we're going? How likely is an avalanche?

The hike turns out to be less dramatic than I expected. I realize those chunks of stone aren't going anywhere.

The trail is wide enough for two people, which I prefer over the team-huddle approach. The lookout is spectacular—rows of mountains touching the horizon in every direction. I feel small. It would be easy to get lost.

Coming down, I'm at the back, next to the staff guy, David.

"You're an expert at this Christian stuff, right?" I ask. He must be, if he's leading our group.

"I don't know about *expert*," he says seriously, "but I've learned a few things over the years. Why do you ask?"

"I was hoping you could explain the Trinity. Katherine talked about it today, but Sunday School was years ago. Kinda in one ear, out the other... you know. I'm pretty new at this faith thing."

"That's what I'm here for," he says. I get the impression he enjoys questions. "What is it you'd like to know, exactly?"

"Well, Katherine thinks the Trinity is the cat's pajamas," I begin, and that gets a laugh from David. "Something changes in her voice when she talks about it... them... those guys. I can't see what she's so excited about, though."

"I think you're right about that," he says. "Do you know what the word Trinity means?"

"Yes. God is one but three: Father, Son, and Spirit. They're different, but the same, or something. *Tri* means three, as in tricycle, and unity refers to oneness. Three in one."

"You *were* paying attention in Sunday School," he says. "Hold on a minute while I put this headlamp on. Okay, that's better. Back to the Trinity. It's not an easy concept, but the Trinity helps us understand everything else. God is three distinct persons, existing in a profound unity of love, values, and purpose. So much so, it's said that they live as one."

"Okay, that's kinda what I heard in Sunday School. There was talk about clovers and St. Patrick too. But what I don't grasp is why it's important for my life."

"Many Christians don't have a clue why the Trinity matters," David says. "They are convinced it's too confusing, and they never think about it again."

"Yep to that." I nod.

"Let me ask you this—What do you think God's life was like before He created the universe?"

"Before people?" I ask.

"Yes, before people, angels, or Satan. What was that life like? When you imagine Father, Son, and Spirit, what are they doing?"

"What are they doing? I don't know. Playing harps and stuff?" I pretend to play a harp in the air, but it's dark, and David can't see. "Sounds boring."

"Boring. Exactly! Just like all moms and dads had boring lives before kids came along, correct?" He pauses to let it sink in. "Children have a very narrow perception of reality beyond themselves. Trust me, Mom and Dad had lots to do before kids showed up. One could argue it's the kids who make life boring."

"True. I hadn't thought about it like that before," I confess. "Then what do you think God was doing before He made us?"

"I would suggest God did the same things then that He does now: communicate, create, love, think, enjoy relationship, appreciate beauty, encourage, give... should I keep going?" he asks.

"Uh... I don't know. It's a bit abstract."

"Yeah, I'll give you that. Have you thought much about what God is like as a person: as a being who has a life outside your existence?"

"Can't say I have." No wonder they keep it simple in Sunday School.

"The Bible affirms we are made in God's image.[70] Our ability to feel and think and choose comes from Him. He created us to be like Him in these ways. If we can love, surely God has always been capable of love. If we are created for relationship, surely God had relationship before He made humans."

"That makes sense. God made us to be like Him, to follow His example. That's why He's a good teacher." I think of watching my sister Katie show her daughter how to eat with a spoon last weekend.

"Love always wants to serve and bless the other," David adds.

"So... they took turns bringing each other coffee in the morning and washing the car on Saturday?" That's an interesting mental picture.

"I can't vouch for the exact details... but the heart of what you describe is bang on. Love always wants to give. Love pays attention to the other. Love affirms. Love helps and cares for others. God doesn't interact with the physical world in the same way we do—drinking coffee and taking naps—but love and communication apply to the Trinity as well as to us."

I see a flash of headlamps ahead and realize we've reached the parking lot.

"Can we finish this conversation back at the centre?" David asks. "I'm the driver, and multitasking is not one of my talents."

"Sure thing," I reply.

***

I find David drinking tea on the stone patio, looking at the stars.

"Are you sure I'm not keeping you up too late?" I ask.

"Not at all! Talking theology is much better than sleep," he replies.

"Cool. Our talk was getting rather interesting," I say. I thought about God's life before people on the drive back. I could learn a lot about life from how Father, Son, and Spirit interact with each other.

"Yes, interesting is a great description for the life of the Trinity. Listen to this quote by Dallas Willard." He pulls a notecard from his Bible and reads:

> We should, to begin with, think that God leads a very interesting life, and that He is full of joy. Undoubtedly He is the most joyous

being in the universe… All of the good and
beautiful things from which we occasionally
drink tiny droplets of soul-exhilarating joy,
God continuously experiences in all their
breadth and depth and richness.[71]

"I love that," David says. "God experiences joy
and beauty and creativity to a degree we don't realize.
Remember the view at the lookout? He made that!"

"What I don't quite get is why God made us in
the first place," I venture. "If those guys had an
amazing, joyous life, why bother with us? We've done
a crappy job loving them back."

"Another good question," David agrees. "A
couple can be happy with each other and still hope for a
child. As they consider having a baby, they realize the
relationship with him or her will be one-directional for
a long time. The child will be helpless and needy.
Despite the sacrifice it will require, they choose to share
their love beyond themselves."

"I wish I could view God in a parental way, but
divorce has messed up my ability to see family as
positive."

"I see. It is a challenge for kids of divorce to
experience God as He really is." David pauses to refill
his tea. "Should I keep going?"

I nod.

"God is unlimited in love. He wants to share life
with others. He dreams of all people participating in the
relationship that exists between Father, Son, and Spirit.
He wants all of us to experience His delight and His
affection. There is room at His table for all of us."

"Okay, I get it: God loves and takes care of us
like a parent because we're so needy and He's got it all
together. But why bother with the relationship between

the three of them? Why do they need each other when they have everything?" I ask.

"Isn't that the mystery of the universe... why have relationship at all?"

"Huh?" It's been a long day for me.

"Tell me about your best friend," he requests.

Unexpected change of topic. Okay. "I have two best friends: Nav and Adrian. They're the guys who know me best."

"Are they weak and pitiful types, or men you respect and look up to?" he asks.

"Let's just say I wouldn't mind being a bit more like them," I answer.

"They're not overly demanding or pitiful?"

"Nope—just average."

"And you like being together?"

I nod.

"You can hang out without an agenda?"

"Yeah."

"You go out of your way to be with them?"

"Yes."

"Well, there you have it—friendship between equals. What is sweeter than sharing life together, even when you don't need anything?"

"So the same thing that motivates me hang out with Nav and Adrian is what motivates the Trinity?" I ask.

"Now you see what I'm talking about," he says with satisfaction. "I did a Bible study on how the Trinity speak about each other. When you read what they say about each other, it sounds a bit like they're bragging on each other. There's a deep appreciation and respect between them."

"Can you give an example?" I ask.

"For sure... at Jesus's baptism, a dove comes from heaven, and everyone hears the Father saying,

'This is my son; with him I am well pleased.'[72] On the mount of transfiguration, the Father declares, 'This is my son; listen to him.'[73]

"When Jesus talks about His Father, He says, 'In my Father's house, there are many dwelling places.'[74] In the Lord's Prayer, Jesus goes on and on about how great the Father is: the kingdom is His, the power is His, He gets the glory.[75] When Jesus mentions Spirit, He's full of confidence and pride: 'When the Spirit of truth comes, He will lead you into *all* truth and teach you everything.'[76]

"They're not trying to take credit for themselves. They're not insecure. They keep pointing back to one another. They're not worried about being forgotten. They are confident in their relationship. They adore each other."

"It would be nice to have friends like that," I say. And it's true. I like my friends, but I don't have the same kind of excitement about them that David's describing.

"Yes, it sure would," he says grinning. "And that, my friend, is why Katherine gets excited about the Trinity. God has always lived in community. He's always been relational. He's always considered others. He's always understood the importance of distinctness in the midst of unity."

"You've lost me again, David," I admit. It's too late to pretend I understand him.

"The bottom line is, God values each individual as a unique entity. He's not trying to squeeze us into one huge blob of sameness. He's not the Borg, for goodness' sake! Just think about it—you can't have a healthy relationship without distinctness. Each member of the Trinity has maintained uniqueness, and God honours the parts of you that make you you. Each person must have freedom of opinion, the choice of how and when to open up, and the option to draw back from a relationship. Healthy relationships are like dancing—the tension of drawing close and pulling back display its beauty.[77]

"As a relational being Himself, it's logical that God would create beings who possess this capacity for relationship. Since God has infinite love, it would be a pity not to share it. There is nothing more important to God than relationship."

"Then all the messed-up relationships out there must kill Him," I say. "He's got to know how much my parents hate each other."

"I think you're right. He, of all beings, fully appreciates the beauty of relationship and the value of each individual. He grieves the most when people and relationships are broken."

"Is it true the Bible says that God hates divorce?"

"Yes, it's in there. Malachi chapter two, verse sixteen."

"Well, I hate it too," I say.

David nods in agreement.

"I think I gotta hit the hay," I say, standing up. "Thanks for this, David; you've given me lots to think about."

"You're welcome, Manuel." He reaches out to shake my hand. "Father, Son, and Spirit adore you and are pleased to have all of eternity to spend with you! See you in the morning."

"Night."

Chapter Fourteen

> You turned on your own feelings. Since feelings
> are so painful, you damped them down…
> Feelings hurt, you said to yourself. So I won't
> have them. It worked for many years. Bad news
> or good news, you felt invulnerable.[78]

Tuesday, 8:58 am

Sloane

Day Two: What to Do with Them Emotions?

We took thirty minutes to sing worship songs and reflect on Scripture verses together. I'm not musical, but it's fun to hear live music and get a bit of singing into my day. I like hearing the connections others make between the songs and Scripture and what we've discussed.

I'm curious what the guys did last night. Did they drink hot chocolate and try on clothes? Whatever they did must have been a hit, because I picked up a happy vibe at breakfast this morning.

Katherine puts an image of Maslow's hierarchy of needs on the screen, and I flash back to Grade Ten social studies.[79] The diagram is pyramid-shaped, with five layers. The bottom layer is **physiological needs**: food, water, shelter, clothing. The next layer is **safety and security**: health, property, family, and social stability. On top of that is **love and belonging**: friendship, family, intimacy, and a sense of connection. On top of that is **self-esteem**: confidence, respect of others, the need to be a unique individual. At the very top of the pyramid is **self-actualization**: morality,

139

creativity, acceptance, meaning, and inner potential. Each layer is built on the layers below it.

She reviews the chart and explains less than fifty percent of children from divorced families say they generally felt safe when they were growing up.[80]

"What this means is, ten or more of you in this room did not feel safe as a child. Take a moment to consider your childhood. How safe did you feel? Consider both the physical and emotional realms. *Safe* implies the perception of security, the ability to trust and depend on life, a freedom from worry and anxiety, little fear of danger or injury.

"Many of you did not grow up with a strong foundation of security and trust. You have been struggling to move beyond this level," she points to the chart. "You are trying to create something you did not have and to compensate for what was lacking in your family. You may not even know what you are aiming for, which makes it all the more complex.

"However, I am confident you can grow. God wants to restore what has been lost, though it doesn't happen magically. Growth and change demand much from you. One myth about success is that good intentions will do the trick—but there's more to it than that."[81]

She walks to the sound system and hits play. Jazz music. Percussion, piano, saxophone. I have to smile. Katherine's tapping her foot, and delight is written on her face. I like seeing this side of her. (Later she tells us the song is Dave Bruebek's famous "Take Five."[82])

"Come with me for a minute," she says when the song is over. She leads us to the hallway.

We follow her to a small room full of musical instruments. "I'm giving you two hours of good effort to recreate the song we heard." She checks her watch.

"I've invited the staff for a lunchtime concert—so get to it.

"Any takers?" The silence stretches until she cracks a smile. "I didn't think so. I don't actually expect this of you… and do you know why?" She looks at us with raised eyebrows.

She picks up a saxophone from the stand and plays the solo we just heard. We hoot in appreciation and amazement.

"I don't expect this from you…" she says, out of breath, "because it's stinking hard to play sax. I've been working on it for twelve years!

"Success takes more than *trying* hard. You have to learn the right way to do something. Once you learn, you have to practice over and over again. You need someone to correct what you're doing wrong, and eventually, if you don't give up, you get better. Whether it is playing saxophone, dealing with anger, or sensing God's love, effort is not enough… but it is a good place to start.

"I practiced an hour a day for a year before anything like music came out of this baby. Most people never get that far. They try for a week or two, get discouraged, then decide it is impossible.

"Some habits you learned as a child were necessary then. But now those exact habits hold you back. Trying to change your feelings does not work. You can't push-start a stalled car from the inside. You must learn new ways of thinking—new ways of seeing the world. Until you change your thinking, nothing will change in your life."

We return to the classroom and watch a video by a pastor called John Ortberg about the difference between trying and training.[83] One example I can relate to is how most people can't run a marathon simply by trying hard without any training. But many people can run a marathon if they train *and* try hard.

If we expect success to be instant, no wonder we get discouraged and disillusioned so often. I couldn't have run those 10Ks without a lot of training and a lot of hard work.

***

During our thirty-minute break before the next session, I head outside and find a trail going uphill. If you start with going up, the way back home is more fun.

I am guilty of quitting whatever activity I can't excel at. I've lost track of everything I've quit. Figure skating. Ukrainian. Handball. Irish dancing. Gymnastics. Swim team.

Somehow I accepted what Pastor John explained in the video—the idea that trying hard will make everything easy. When reality does not match my expectations, I feel like a complete failure. I can't handle looking foolish, or being laughed at. I'd rather stay where I am than risk ridicule.

I wonder what I've missed out on because of my fear? What if I'd learned to dance, to swim, to speak Ukrainian, to skate, to play the viola? Why can't I stick with anything? Why am I so afraid?

***

Katherine is standing in the middle of the room when we return from the break. Everything has been rearranged. The tables and chairs are set up in a big ring around the outside of the room.

"Today we are going to talk about emotions," she says. "A common trait of children of divorce is an inability to identify and express emotions. You've got them, but you have learned to hide or ignore the ones you're not comfortable with. Some emotions were permitted in your family. Some were prohibited. Most of us have a few favorites—anger, loneliness, fear, or something else.

"God created you with the whole spectrum of emotions. Emotions help you live deeply and authentically. Until you can experience all of them, you miss out on being fully human. You are hindered in experiencing God's love for you.[84]

"It can be frightening or uncomfortable to talk about emotions and to access them. We are going to tread lightly today and be very kind to each other.

"Emotions are peculiar. They can surprise you with their intensity and sudden appearance. At times they are welcome visitors, and alternately, they can be stubborn guests who refuse to leave. As soon as someone says the word 'dentist,' I feel panic. However, I have learned to acknowledge my emotions and respond to them so they cannot control me. I experience fear and anxiety about the dentist, but I get in my car and go to the appointment anyway.

"Emotions are a response to something—internal or external, real or imaginary. [85] Realizing where they come from doesn't always make them go away, but this allows you to lessen their power over you.

"I've discovered it's counterproductive to debate an emotion. What I mean is, telling myself, 'I do not feel angry' or 'Stop feeling angry' when I'm angry is pointless. I might not be able to describe what I feel, but the feelings are real. I cannot talk myself out of an emotion. I tried for years. Emotions are your body's way of getting your attention. Emotions are God's messengers to us, and it's wise to notice what they communicate."

We will have two hours to visit "stations" set up around the room. Each station explores an emotion, and there are art supplies, Scripture verses, activities, and questions for us to ponder.

"There is no need to rush through the stations," she instructs. "Memories, events, or people might come to mind that are not directly connected to the stations. Pay attention to your feelings and let them guide you."

We spread out to the stations, and quiet music starts playing. It's hard to describe how I feel. Excitement, anger, confusion, and fear are all there. I make sure I know where the door is in case I want to leave.

***

Rachel's Journal

Where can I sign up for emotion lessons? How are we supposed to learn about them? There's so much I don't know about them. I didn't learn jack about emotions… or about communication… as a kid. They frighten and confuse me.

I wish I had parents like that one amazing couple from church, Lauren and Frank. I remember having dinner with them one night when their six-year-old, Abby, had a meltdown. I got tense, wondering how Frank and Lauren would respond to a crying child. But neither of them got upset. Frank calmly asked what was wrong. Abby explained, "I feel sad because Mommy only gave me two cookies, and I wanted three." Dad leaned in and pulled Abby to his shoulder. She got snot on his shirt but let him comfort her. I heard him say, "I know, it is sad when you don't get something you want." The crisis passed; she picked up her fork and ate her peas.

That would never have happened in my house.

How different my life would be if someone, anyone, had taught me to notice and express my feelings… about cookies and everything else.

***

Kimmie's Journal

Anger is the worst. I hate when people are angry. My heart beats so fast that I freeze. My mouth is glued shut. Angry people push and push until they knock everyone over. Giving in early is the best choice. Don't make a fuss. Give them what they want. Act happy about it.

Even when I've done nothing wrong, a raised voice still sends me running. I panic. I'm eight again, hiding under the couch, hoping no one will see me. I'm thirteen, trying to keep them happy, saying what they want to hear.

How is it I'm an adult but *feel* like a child?

In Grade Three, my friend Sarah skipped four months of school to travel with her family. She missed history and math and a unit about China. I always went to school, but it feels like I missed the lessons where you learn about conflict and harmony and not being afraid.

Is there any way to take those lessons now?

***

Jenn's Journal

I feel like my life is made of crumbs. Torn up bread fallen on the floor. I made no sound. I had no voice.

I'm the leftover bits no one wants. I was insignificant. I got the leftovers of both parents… and step-parents. The best was reserved for the "real kids," the ones who lived there full-time.

Children love to be found during Hide and Seek, but what do you call the feeling when no one notices you're hiding?
At one point, they fought over me. But after that, it was neglect and resentment. How ironic.

No one took me to the playground or watched my volleyball games. No one had time for crafts or baking cookies. In my new houses, there were strict rules. Everything had a place… and there was no place for crumbs or leftovers.

***

If there is any single experience that unites children of divorce, it is our feelings of loneliness as children.[86]

***

Brad's Journal

A few years before Mom and Dad split up, we went to Jasper for a vacation. I remember watching the mountains grow big on the horizon.

I double-checked and triple-checked my seatbelt to make sure it was fastened. I felt happy and small, in a good way, as we drove along. Sunlight warmed me, and a breeze from the front window tickled my face.

We'd turn a corner on the mountain road, and suddenly I'd be looking down the steep drop-off. I'd beg my brother to switch, but he never would. I'd imagine the door opening, my seatbelt unbuckling, and a helplessness as I'd tumble over the edge.

I never knew if Dad and Mom were scared on that road. I couldn't see their faces from the back seat.

Whenever I'm afraid, I think of that twisty road. I remember the fear in my stomach, my anger at my brother, my anger at Mom and Dad for not noticing I was terrified.

Is there anyone who cares how I feel?

***

Melissa's Journal

I don't care what Katherine says. I have done a good job controlling my emotions and talking myself through them. For example, sadness is easy to deal with—just don't go there. There are lots of things to be happy about. Sadness serves no purpose.

I choose gratitude. I'm strong. Crying doesn't change anything.

I shut the door whenever sadness comes knocking. Whenever it gets close, I change the channel.

Things are quiet inside of me, and I like that. That's what I aim for—keep everything outside, and let nothing in.
I spend most of life feeling nothing, and it's an okay way to feel.[87]

***

Matt's Journal

I feel bitter about the life I've been given— sorry, Gandalf. It's like a kid born in summertime. No one throws a party for you if you're born in summer. No one brings cupcakes to school to share. There's no special day when people notice you.

It's unfair that I didn't get what the other kids had. They got clowns and presents, and I got nothing. That's my life. No home. No place where I fit. No one who understands my worlds.
I'm always a spectator in someone else's celebration.

No one witnesses my life. No one defends me. No one explains why it is the way it is.

***

Jake's Journal

I have a vivid, reoccurring dream about Christmas. The biggest gift under the tree has my name on it, and I'm so excited!

I open my gift slowly, without tearing the paper, just the way Grandma does. Beneath the paper I see brown cardboard. No hints about what's inside.

Maybe every gift I asked for that year is packed into one big box?

I open the lid, but inside the box there is nothing. Nothing at all. I turn it upside down and shake it. It must be a trick. A puzzle.

I ask every relative and guest for help. I yell, pull sleeves, stamp my feet, shake shoulders. No one can hear me or see me.

I am invisible.
That's when I wake up.
It's a horrible dream.

***

148

We heard… how divorce pushes young people into anxiety. This anxiety causes them to doubt the dependability of the universe or to wonder whether we are anything but a shadow within it.[88]

***

Manuel's Journal

Happiness has become very complicated for me. Most people chase after happiness, but for me it's tainted by guilt and loneliness. When I celebrated with Dad, I felt guilty because Mom wasn't there. When there was good news, I had to decide who I'd tell first and prepare myself to absorb the anger of the other parent's offence.

If there was ever something good for me, unconnected to either of them, I didn't know how to feel happy. Somehow they owned my happiness, and I don't know how to get it back.

***

For children of divorce, to gain one parent *always* means to lose the other. Over time we became divided, torn between two worlds. Exile is a spiritual name for our feeling of inner division. It helps explain our sense of being fragmented, spread out, scattered.[89]

***

Sloane's Journal

I read one children's book about divorce. Writers assume children are dumb and materialistic. Life is not better now that we have two bedrooms, two bikes, or two houses.

The character in the book was meant to resemble a twenty-first century Goldilocks. Isn't she cute, with two beds and two bowls of porridge and never a fear that bears might chase her! Gag me.

As an adult, the terrifying irony of the story dawned on me. In the original Goldilocks, the girl searches for items that are "just right" for her. The girl from the divorced family is not like Goldilocks at all. This girl can't go where she likes. She's not the hero of the story but another object, like the bed or chair or bowl of porridge. She's the thing Mom and Dad rejected in their search for what was "just right" for them.

It's horrible to be the rejected object of any of story, left behind by characters who didn't give a backward glance.

***

Children are frightened and angry, terrified of being abandoned by both parents, and they feel responsible for the divorce. Most children are taken by surprise; few are relieved... They recall how they were expected to adjust overnight to a terrifying number of changes that confounded them.[90]

***

Connor's Journal

When I was a kid, Mom explained that our stomachs made us throw up to clean out something bad that got inside. Even though it's horrible to puke, it actually keeps you from staying sick.

I wish it was so easy to clean out feelings. I have years of horrible feelings trapped inside of me. Some of the worst are what I'd feel when I saw Mom with her boyfriend. They laughed and whispered to each other like I wasn't in the room. I tried to block it out, but I can't erase it. I don't want that feeling stuck inside of me.

No wonder my stomach hurt so much back then.

***

Jason's Journal

I've been left behind on an island, stranded by the crew.

For a while, I could see a ship on the horizon. It gave me hope, hope of a someday rescue. But now the ship is gone. I can't see it, and it can't see me. It's never coming back.

I am totally alone, and no one is looking for me.

Chapter Fifteen

Tuesday, 5:18 pm

Manuel

> Contrary to what we have long thought, the major impact of divorce does not occur during childhood or adolescence. Rather, it rises in adulthood as serious romantic relationships move to center stage. When it comes time to choose a life mate and build a new family, the effects of divorce crescendo.[91]

***

There's time to kill before dinner. From the balcony of my room, I see Connor sitting outside on the grass. I grab my water bottle and walk to the lawn.

"Hey, Connor. Mind if I join you?" I ask.

"Not at all. Soaking up the view while I can."

"I still can't believe I'm here. This is amazing," I agree. "Can I bug you with a question?"

"Shoot."

"Yesterday you mentioned you have a girlfriend. I wanted to ask about that... I mean... this seems like a good place to ask for advice." Connor's good-looking and seems to have his act together. He must have some advice for me. "I've had a hard time with girlfriends... finding them... keeping them. I wonder what it's been like for you. Can you help out a brother?"

"I'm not sure I can help, but I don't mind the question. If we don't talk about it, who will?"

I knew he was the right one to ask.

"I've been with Megan for a year," Connor continues. "We met at work when I noticed her reading the Bible at lunch. You gotta be pretty serious with God to bring a Bible to the office. She was friendly, and it wasn't long before I asked her out."

"Cool."

"Yeah, it was," he says, but he doesn't sound excited. "She's from 'the other side'—her parents are happily married, and so are her older sisters. It's intimidating, to be honest."

"Do you think you guys'll get married?" I ask.

"It's hard to say. We both have fears about marriage. Mine from what I saw growing up. Megan's uncomfortable with the stats about children of divorce—how likely we are to get divorced and stuff like that. We got in a fight about it the night before I came here."

"That's rough timing for a fight," I say with a whistle. "Is it messing with your head?"

"I wish it wasn't, but yeah. Apparently her parents are 'concerned.' They're basically asking her, 'Why exactly does your boyfriend need a week of intense counseling?'" he says, "I thought they'd be happy I'm dealing with things instead of blowing them off. It sucks to be labeled."

"Dude, that's brutal," I say. "People think it's contagious, right?"

Connor sighs. I feel bad for the guy.

"Watch out, world!" I stretch out my arms and make a zombie face. "Child of divorce on the loose, coming to ruin your perfect family!"

Connor laughs.

"What are you going to do about Megan?" I ask.

"Not sure. Part of me wants to end it. I'm starting to feel I'm on trial all the time. What do they want from me?" Connor sighs again. "On the other hand, I'm glad she's stuck with me for a year."

"So you have no clue what you're gonna do."

"Sure don't." Connor throws a pebble across the grass. "I know it's important, but I don't want to spend this whole week thinking about Megan. There's deeper stuff I need to work on, you know?"

"Yeah. That's good, man." There had to be something positive to say.

"You know what I wish, Manuel?"

"What?"

"I wish it wasn't so hard. Why can't I just meet a woman with a 'soulmate' sign and know she's the one? I'd like to share life with someone, but so far it hasn't happened. Do you think it's even possible?"

I take a moment to think before responding, "I would like it to be." And that's the truth.

***

The absence of a good image negatively influences their search for love, intimacy, and commitment. Anxiety leads many into making bad choices in relationships, giving up hastily when problems arise, or avoiding relationships altogether.[92]

***

Tuesday, 5:33 pm

Sloane

Rachel and I are crashed on our beds. We have time before dinner, and I'd rather be in my room than hanging with a crowd. I am half-asleep, face down on my pillow, when I hear her stirring.

"You conscious over there, Sloane?" she asks.

"Maybe," I say into the pillow.

"Can I ask you something?"

"Uh-hm."

"Does it seem odd to you how old we are?"

"We're old…?"

"Not you and me specifically, but all of us. Are we behind the ball, the dull tacks in the box? I mean, why has it taken so long for us to get where we are now?"

I do a mental review of the group and the people who meet at Sal's. I roll over to look at her. "I hadn't thought about it. I'm not sure, actually. I've only been dealing with this stuff for a few months."

"Yeah, me too. I started counseling in January… Last Christmas was a nightmare."

"What's odd to me," I say, "is I've gone my whole life never bringing up the divorce, and now, out of the blue, groups and retreats and books appear all over the place."

"Maybe God sets us up when He knows we can handle it," she suggests.

"So it's a positive thing we've realized our lives are messed up?" I ask.

"We might as well get with the program." She pauses and fluffs her pillow. "It reminds me of what they do with burn victims, you know, keep them in a coma while their body is healing."

I puff up my pillow too. "Wait, are you saying I've *been* in a coma, or I'm *still* in a coma?"

"Heck—what do I know?" she says with a laugh. "All I'm saying is I sure hope God knows what He's doing, because I'm as confused as ever."

Tuesday, 8:42 pm

I forgot how cold the evenings get in the mountains, even in summer. The crisp air makes the stars and moon seem even closer. I'm glad I grabbed a flannel shirt and socks from the room before heading to the firepit.

I survived another day, and no one's driving me crazy yet. I actually like our group.

Campfires are magical. Once you're staring at one, you never want to leave. Add the smell of toasted marshmallows and the sound of the logs crackling: *ahhhh*. Everyone looks good in the glow of the flames. I like how soothing they are.

David plays a few songs on the guitar (not *Kumbaya*). You can't beat music around a campfire, either. David has a voice made for radio—deep and captivating. He puts the guitar down and talks about Adam and Eve living in the Garden of Eden. Before Adam and Eve ate the fruit and things got messed up, God would walk with them in the cool of the evening.[93] No agenda, no work assignments, no exams about garden regulations. Just friends enjoying the end of a beautiful day together.

I like the image he describes. I wish I had friends like that—sitcom friends who are always together, talking about life and laughing at one another's jokes.

"What if God were here at the campfire with us tonight," David asks, "hanging out, sitting with us, staring at the stars? What would it be like to share a blanket with Him?"

I've never thought about God sitting around a campfire before. If He could hang out with Adam and Eve in a garden, why can't He hang out with us in the mountains?

David heads inside after that, joking how old people need more sleep than us youngsters. He suggests we imagine God walking beside us when we go inside tonight, God sitting on the edge of the bed as we crawl in, God staying there while we sleep, maybe pulling up a chair next to us.

It's been years since I imagined Jesus at my bedside. He used to chase away bad dreams and scary monsters. Maybe He'll keep me company tonight.

Chapter Sixteen

Divorce is like death without a burial.

As children of divorce, we experienced incredible loss: the loss of stability, the loss of financial security, the loss of continuity, the loss of shared history, and the loss of deep intimacy with both parents. Sometimes we lose even the freedom to express this feeling of loss. We also experience a loss of innocent trust when it comes to love and marriage.[94]

Wednesday, 9:03 am

Sloane

Day Three: Tell Me What I've Lost, So It Can be Found

Everything has been rearranged again in the meeting room. Drapes cover the windows, and the décor is dark and subdued. The orange and pink flowers have been replaced with potted plants.

Katherine looks like she's ready for a day at the office—a black business suit replaces her regular, flowing skirt.

"Today's topic—grief and loss—doesn't get a lot of air time in our culture," she begins. "You have experienced deep pain, but you have grown up being told this pain is normal.[95] You have adjusted to living with and ignoring your pain. You have lost sensitivity. You have been hit with loss after loss and have taken it in stride.

"I've met hundreds of children of divorce, and only a small percentage ever talk about the divorce with anyone. Most have no clear idea why the divorce happened. Most aren't sure how the divorce impacted their lives. Most try to live as though it never happened at all. Many feel talking about the divorce is pointless. Most were never approached by an adult, pastor, or relative offering to discuss what happened.

"We live in a culture where divorce has become common. *Common* is what we call situations that aren't too serious and aren't a big deal—the 'common cold,' for example. But divorce is a big deal, and it has become very common.

"Children of divorce are more likely to describe their childhood as lonely, full of anger, and riddled with anxiety. Children of divorce are less likely to trust others or to have hope for the future. Many children of divorce did not feel emotionally or physically safe in their homes.[96] Many have a difficult time articulating *home* at all; they are not sure where they belong.

"You know this already. You have an experiential awareness of these facts. You may not understand what you feel or where these ideas came from, but you've told me divorce is horrible.

"Children of divorce say the day their parents divorced was the day their childhood ended.[97] Your parents said they loved you, but understandably you were confused by what that meant.[98] The greatest pain you've experienced was caused voluntarily by the people you loved the most.

"Many children of divorce believe things will improve when they grow up and are on their own, only to be surprised when things get worse instead of better in adulthood. Children of divorce have taken their pain and loss and tried to absorb it into their being. They have tried to hide it. Over time, this approach eats them up.

"Divorce shapes your perception of the nature of relationships, the world, God, yourself, and your existence. There are cracks in the foundation of who you are, and as you attempt to build on that foundation, the cracks grow larger."

"You have spent much of your life adapting to change and getting by. You have survived much, but as long as you live in the state of 'getting by,' you will not enjoy the abundant life God wants to give you. 'Getting by' does not have to be your fate.

"And this brings us to grief. Grieving has helped me deal with the losses in my life."

Katherine puts up this quote from Dr. Townsend:

> One of the most important processes in life is grief. God has designed grief to help us get over things. When bad things happen in life, we have to work through them. Working through bad things is a little like digesting food. In life, we basically digest experience; we walk through it, take it in, use what is useful, and eliminate the waste.[99]

After reading it, we discuss it for a few minutes with a neighbor.

"I've noticed there are certain types of pain we are reluctant to acknowledge," Katherine comments. "But babies are different—they scream at the slightest discomfort.

"If we were in a car accident, we could identify and discuss our injuries. But when it comes to emotional pain, we often stay quiet. Shame, pride, and fear of hurting those we love are some motivators behind our silence.

"But until we acknowledge the pain and grieve it, we stay trapped. You can be twenty-five or thirty but stuck at the emotional maturity of an eight-year-old who experienced great trauma. We need to give ourselves permission to mourn, and it will take more than one really good crying session.[100]

"Today, we hope to shed light on what has happened to you and to create space for the grieving process. The process will be different for each of you, but I trust Holy Spirit to meet you where you are now.

"This evening we will have a memorial service to mark what you have lost through divorce. Your chosen outfit has been delivered to your room."

***

If grief is the answer to so many of life's problems, why don't we just do it? We usually hold funerals only when someone dies, but we also need to grieve other things. The problem is that we don't often see those experiences as losses. So we stay in denial or protest for a long time.[101]

***

Evan explains that one of the first traumas for children of divorce is the disorientation of change. It begins when children are told about the divorce. Parents, not wanting to dwell on the pain of the break-up, often downplay what is happening. They don't mention their grief over the failed marriage. They don't discuss the emotional distress or the abuse motivating the divorce.

Many parents adopt a no-nonsense approach, describing the divorce like a business transaction. As soon as they hear the news, children perceive there is little room for questions, outbursts, dialogue, or sadness. From the child's perspective, the divorce has come out of nowhere, and everything bad is swept under the carpet, leaving him or her in a state of shock.[102] The decision has been made—without them—and the show must go on.

What explanation were we given for the divorce? Evan asks us to write what we were told on big sheets of paper, which he hangs on the wall.[103]

- *They never told me. When Dad didn't come home one day, my mom refused to talk to me about it.*
- *Adultery. My dad cheated multiple times, which led to a pregnancy with another woman, which led to the divorce.*
- *They didn't explain; we just moved out. Later on, I realized it was because Mom was an addict.*
- *They didn't love each other for a long time. They weren't happy. My dad said it was my sister's and my fault—if we'd cleaned more or got along better, they would still be together.*
- *Mom said, "Your dad and I don't love each other anymore." Later on we found out she was having an affair, and when she left us, she moved in with the guy.*
- *They never gave an answer, but when they were drunk, they liked to tell me it was my fault.*
- *My mom wanted to be free from the responsibility of marriage and motherhood.*
- *My mom was unhappy and fell out of love with my dad.*
- *Too much hurt between them. They loved each other but couldn't be together.*
- *My father had a sudden change of heart about having a family. Although he initially wanted children, once my mother was getting close to*

having me, he lost interest.
- *My dad was an alcoholic and wanted that more than us.*
- *They said it was a mutual decision.*

On the other walls are drawings made by kids in the early days after their parents' divorce. We walk around, looking at them like we're in an art gallery. It's heartbreaking to see how these children have perceived and expressed what happened.

I'm transported back to the day I found out about the divorce. The details are still vivid. When I see seven-year-olds now, I'm shocked by how small and helpless they are, utterly unequipped to deal with that volume of pain. How can anyone say divorce isn't a big deal?

***

Katherine is sitting on one of the couches at the back of the room and we find seats nearby. She reads a poem about mourning. It's longish and sort of confusing (like all poetry), but it's describing how the author feels love and sadness and anger and exhaustion, all at the same time. She doesn't say so, but I think she wrote it.

Amy shows us one of her drawings. It's dark with shadows and jagged lines. I don't know what it means (I don't get art either), but she speaks slowly, explaining the loss and loneliness and fear she felt when she was drawing. I want to applaud for her.

Our assignment for the afternoon is to reflect on the losses we've experienced. They give us a list of categories and some questions to think about. We're supposed to be brutally honest with God and ourselves. *Don't edit yourself*, they say. *There's no one you're trying to impress, and God already knows how you feel.*

This activity is part of preparing the presentations we'll give at the memorial service tonight. The staff is around for consultation if we need help.

I knew they'd make us do hard stuff.

Chapter Seventeen

Wednesday, 6:48 pm

Sloane

It's weird to get dressed up for the memorial of a thing instead of a person. It's weird to have a memorial for a thing, period. Funerals are stressful.

After stubbing some toes and an altercation with the straightener, Rachel puts on 90s pop to improve our mood.

The meeting room is arranged like a lecture hall—chairs in rows and a podium at front. I notice boxes of Kleenex. I won't need them—I'm not much of a crier. People are milling around, folding and unfolding their printed speeches. We do clean up nice, I have to admit.

David welcomes us and explains that we can give our speeches in whatever order we like. Jake's the eager beaver who walks up front first. He clears his throat and unfolds his paper.

Jake's Speech

As a child, there was a dream I always wanted to have, but my subconscious refused to cooperate.

In my dream, I had a superpower. I would climb on my bed, pull the covers over me, and the bad things of that day—falling in a mud puddle at recess, throwing up in math, you name it—would magically be undone when I pulled the covers down again.

The day I wanted to undo more than any other was the day Dad told me he and Mom were getting divorced.

Today, I remember when Mom and Dad were married; I remember the years I could be a child and trust someone to take care of me. I remember the life I had before I needed a superpower to make it through.

Today, before you all, I acknowledge what I have lost. The day my parents divorced is the day I lost the sense of being safe and loved. On that day, I said goodbye to a world where I was taken care of, and I entered a world where I was the one who had to care for others. Gone was the simplicity of grass stains and spelling tests. The divorce stole my carefree life, my innocent childhood, my confidence that the world was a good place. I entered a fearful world where no one was to be trusted.

Mom and Dad did not always use their powers for good. They were the ones who hurt me the most, though they didn't realize it. Determined to get what they wanted—a fresh start, new love, release from an unhappy marriage—they were blind to the pain they caused.

Today, I remember my eight years with a whole family, my eight years of being their little boy. Losing that security has been the most difficult thing. Even today, I'm not sure who I can trust.

Mom and Dad, I forgive you. You didn't anticipate how much your choice would touch me, or that I wouldn't be able to tell you what was going on inside. I never knew how to tell you what I felt.

I wish I had lived in a world where I didn't need a superpower to survive, and I grieve the safe life I lost.

Thank you.

***

We clap for Jake and hug him as he walks back to his seat. Rachel gets up while we are still clapping and makes her way to the front.

Rachel's Speech

To prepare for the memorial service today, I had to ask myself some questions: about family, about love, about home.

It's challenging to describe what I lost, because I don't know what I might have had. What is it like to breathe air? How do you describe gravity? What does a "together family" feel like?

People tell me there are no perfect families, and I'm sure that's true. There are always fights and hurts and things you want to change.

For me, family is a phenomenon from another planet. When I try to think of it, I'm a blind person imagining orange or blue. How can I understand what I've never experienced?

Maybe family is like waking up on the first day of summer vacation. The sun is shining, you feel happy, there's no pressure to perform. You feel hopeful and excited.

I didn't have this growing up. *Happy, excited*, and *hopeful* were not words in my vocabulary. Instead of laughter and play, my childhood was an exercise in survival. There was no place for enjoyment or delight or silliness. My childhood was painted in brown and gray.

All sense of belonging and connection was taken from me. I was robbed of identity and safety. The divorce stole love, and it destroyed home.

For years, I said those things didn't matter—they were for other people. But I was wrong. Perhaps family and home and belonging are the answer to the emptiness I know so well. I am afraid I will never learn these things. Perhaps I am so broken I will never know anything different. I am like a blind person, stumbling through life, trying to find what I don't know how to recognize.

It has been a discouraging search. I keep looking, and I hope I'll be able to tell when I find what I long for.

That's it.

***

We clap, and I give Rachel a big hug when she sits back down. I would never guess that's how she feels. People are full of surprises.

Manuel is standing up front by the time I finish congratulating Rachel on her bravery. There are a lot of people who want to get this over with! I don't know him well, but he seems like a decent guy—thoughtful and sincere.

"I haven't been to many funerals," he begins, "but David suggested writing a letter to my parents. I'm pretty nervous, so please bear with me." His voice is trembling. Actually, *he* is trembling. He unfolds his letter and begins to read.

Manuel's Speech

Dear Mom and Dad,

It feels weird to write this letter to both of you, because I can't picture you together in the same place. However, there are some things I want both of you to hear.

You were in love when you got married, and you told me you were in love when I was born. That's comforting on one hand, but distressing on the other.

I've often wondered what changed between my birth and your decision to divorce. How can so much change in so few years?

You said your marriage was challenging. I wonder how hard you tried to keep it together. Did you listen to each other? Did you compromise at all? I'm not sure which answer I'd rather hear—that you tried hard and still couldn't make it work, or that you hardly tried.

Either way, your decision to divorce and try again with someone else really messed up my life. I wish you'd tried harder the first time around. I wish you'd been less willing to give up. Isn't love supposed to stick to its guns? Isn't love supposed to fight for a solution? I feel ashamed that my parents lied when they took their wedding vows.

I don't have any memories of you two being affectionate. Instead, I have images of you making out with people you weren't married to. I wish I could erase them. My perception of romance and sexuality and marriage has been twisted, and I hate that.

I wish I'd grown up in a house where I was loved by both of the adults who lived there. Instead, I felt loved by one and tolerated by the other.[104] I never felt I could be myself in either place. Mom and Dad, I never felt you knew who I was.

Your decision to divorce cast a shadow over my life, and there's no going back. You took from me what no one else can give. I lost years trying to deal with the repercussions of your choices. You took so much from me and never asked permission. I feel anger and bitterness. Now that I'm grown up and on my own, no one understands what I've lost. Everyone expects me to move on, but I don't know how.

Mom and Dad, you have given me life, and I'm grateful. You have watched me grow up, and you have been proud of me. I wish the divorce could have been good for all of us, but twenty-two years later, I want you to know it was bad for me—very bad.

***

Wednesday, 7:32 pm

Sloane

We clap and cheer for Manuel. His smile is a bit sad, but his head is up, and he's not afraid to look us in the eye. I don't cheer for the pain he's expressed or the details of his past, but for his courage to speak it out, to be so honest, to be so raw before us.

I might as well go now. I'm sitting near the front, and before I can talk myself out of it, I'm standing, facing the group.

"Hi, guys," I begin. "I don't know much about funerals, and I'm not a good speaker… but, um… Amy's painting gave me the idea to make something instead of talking." I hold up my poster for everyone to see, then prop it up against a chair next to me. "I'm not artsy, but working on this project helped me think. Amy told me thinking about the topic was more important than how good I sound to everyone."

I search for Amy in the crowd. "What am I supposed to do now…?" I ask.

"Sloane," she says, from a couple rows back, "why don't you tell us what you were thinking while you made this, and explain the different parts."

"Ok, sure." I pick up my poster again. "Well, you guys can see my project here is made out of magazines and garbage and stuff I found in the recycle bin out back. It doesn't smell much, but don't get too close.

"The image of garbage is something I always connect with divorce—getting rid of what you don't want anymore. Divorce gives the message to kids that relationships are disposable. That's what I learned, at least. As a kid, I got used to people disappearing. Mom, relatives, Dad's friends. It became a question of when they would go, not if.

"For some aspects, recycling is a better image. Recycling is when you throw away something that's still good, and someone else uses it. I felt like that... Mom didn't want us kids, so she tossed us away for someone else to make use of.

"Uh, here you see lots of expiration dates from stuff I found. Divorce taught me that relationships have expiration dates. I don't expect anyone to stick around permanently. It would be nice if people were labeled like cartons of milk, but so far I haven't been able to read them that well.

"I cut out some words from a magazine: love, family, commitment, promises. They have expiration dates, too.

"I think this project fits at our memorial because my family didn't last." I shift around uncomfortably, hoping people will look at the project and not at me. "I often feel like garbage, or something that's been thrown in the recycle bin. I might not be totally broken, but no one wants me either.

"Here are some pictures of closed doors. Doors are helpful because they let me escape... or hide. A door gives control over who can be in my life and who can't. The last picture here is also of a door, but this one's open just a bit. You can see some light coming in. I want to open my life up to good things and not always be afraid of what might be waiting on the other side. Thank you."

I sit down but have to get up again so people can hug me. It feels nice to get hugs and smiles and pats on the back instead of silence and apathy.

Now that I've given my talk, it's easier to listen to the others. Each speech is unique and from the heart. It feels odd to sit and listen to so much emotion and so much sadness, but it feels good, too.

I pride myself on being tough, but no one, including me, makes it through the memorial with dry eyes. I never knew attending a lifetime of funerals squeezed into a couple of hours would make me feel exactly like a mashed potato.

***

We basically need two things for grieving. First, we need love, support, and comfort… Second, we need structure… This is why good support groups that meet at a regular time and do regular tasks are effective in getting people through grief.[105]

***

Wednesday, 9:23 pm

When everyone has given their speeches, Katherine tells us to change into our PJs, brush our teeth, and meet back in thirty minutes.

I cannot imagine what we will do thirty minutes from now in our pajamas, but I've stopped worrying about it. These past days have been unusual in every way, but the strange things they've asked us to do have been worth it. Like Connor said, we're here, and we're willing—the rest is up to God.

Wednesday, 9:52 pm

We gather in the meeting room, and after we finish teasing each other (there are some exceptionally nice bunny slippers in the room), Katherine explains what's next.

"When there has been a death in a Jewish community, custom has it the family is not left alone to mourn. Friends and relatives taking turns with the grieving family, letting their presence bring a quality of comfort words alone cannot bring. We tend to hide our sadness and deal with our grief alone, but this tradition teaches us there are some losses we are not strong enough to carry by ourselves.[106]

"Tonight, we are going to camp on the patio. Evan and David have rigged up an elaborate mosquito net to protect us from the bloodsuckers. There are mattresses and blankets and pillows laid out for all of us. Claim your spot, and feel free to turn in when you like. This room will be open all night with snacks and hot drinks, and it is a place to talk and hang out.

"I know we are all a bit old for a sleepover, but being together in the aftermath of grief and mourning is a statement we think it is important to make. We would all probably sleep better in our own beds, but I have discovered being together is sometimes more beneficial for healing than a comfy mattress.

"Let us begin!"

***

Another important reason people cannot grieve the way they need to is that they lack resources... If there is not enough love to sustain us, both inside and out, then we cannot let go of anything, even something bad.[107]

175

Thursday, 12:44 am

Sal

I drink peppermint tea while Katherine finishes up with Rachel. The week is half over, and I'm looking for answers.

"Katherine, thanks for organizing this week. It's been amazing," I say.

"You're welcome. I love doing it," Katherine responds. It's clear to see she does.

"How long do you think they'll keep at it?"

"It's hard to say. This group seems to have a high percentage of night owls."

"I have a few things I'd like to ask you, if that's okay... not from tonight, but more general," I say.

"Definitely," Katherine nods.

"I told you about the Adult Children of Divorce group I host on Fridays, right?"

"Yes, you did. Some people from the group came with you this week."

"Yeah, and it's nice to take a break from leading," I pause. "I've enjoyed the events and activities we've done here, but... please don't take this the wrong way... none of them are super complicated. You make us do all the work."

"Great observation, and I'm not offended at all."

"What I'm curious about is why people find it so hard to talk about their experience. I mean, everyone says it helps once they do it, so why do they put up such a fight?"[108]

"I've noticed that too, and it makes me crazy," Katherine laughs. "Why do you think people struggle to open up?"

"They're afraid of what people will think."

"And…?" Katherine asks.

"They think people will reject them… treat them different if they know what's going on inside," I suggest. "Maybe there's shame, too, like it's only losers who have emotional problems."

"I think those are all part of the puzzle. And when you feel insecure, it's hard to take the risk of exposing more of yourself."

"Right, but Katherine, can't people see how ridiculous that is? Everyone has issues! Why do we waste so much time pretending we don't?" My voice gets louder and louder until I stops myself.

"Sal, I see why people love coming to your group—you're honest and humble and passionate. Don't lose those things." Katherine leans back on the couch. "So let me ask you this; what held you back?"

"Hmmm. Ignorance is bliss, baby… I wasn't thinking about my past or my future in any intentional way. I was crazy busy trying to make rent and do my laundry before I ran out of clean socks. I wouldn't say I was holding back… I didn't even know there was somewhere to go."

"So it wasn't resistance as much as lack of awareness, is that right?"

"Yeah, that's a good way to put it," I say.

"And when did that change?"

"Ah, that's the question. What was my turning point…?" I lean back and rub my forehead. "Well, it wasn't just one thing, but the convergence of a few. I listened to a radio show about the impact of divorce, and I was intrigued. Then a romantic relationship crashed and burned. I blamed the guy but finally clued in that I was the common denominator in my failed relationships. Then an acquaintance raved about a counselor she was seeing, and I decided to make an appointment."

"And did it get sorted out quick and easy?"

"No way! Have you ever tried to get your car out of the ditch, in a blizzard, in the dark, wearing high heels? That would be nothing compared to what I went through."

"Delightful," Katherine chuckles. "How did the counselor help?"

"She gave me assignments. She asked questions I didn't know how to answer. I felt like a blind person being led down a treacherous path. I trusted she knew where to go, but I would have been stuck without her help. It took two years before I really saw changes in my life."

"It's admirable you kept at it, Sal. How did you make it through such an intense time?"

"Mostly my friends at church. There was one family who had the most comfortable couch in the world, perfect for long naps on Sunday afternoons. They acted like counseling was normal. That helped a lot."

"How old were you at this point?" Katherine asks.

"I was in my late twenties when I started counseling. I began the group at my house when I was thirty-one."

"And that's a wrap," Katherine says.

"Huh? A wrap of what?" I ask.

"Sal, you've answered all the questions you came to ask me."

"Really? I did?" I smile. "I'm still thinking clearly at this time of day?"

"Yeah, you are," Katherine laughs. "And I hope you'll remember it all tomorrow. The age and the stage of life when a person opens up will vary. It often happens when an inability to cope comes to light, and there's an example to follow. Connection with a counselor or mentor makes a big difference, as does having a support system. Developmental factors play a role. All in all, I'd say the age range of this group is pretty typical for the work I do."

"I'm glad you're thinking clearly at this time of night yourself," I tease. "I'm going to grab my journal and write down a few of these things, to make sure I do remember them tomorrow… or later today. Thanks very much, Katherine."

Chapter Eighteen

Thursday, 9:00 am

Sloane

Day Four: An Invitation to be Different

Most of us are still dead to the world at nine when David wakes us up with his guitar. Coffee, muffins, and fruit are spread out in the dining room. We're instructed to eat, then get dressed and ready for something outdoors. Hiking boots and sunglasses. I'm getting used to these mysterious trips and surprise adventures. The week feels more and more like an episode of *Survivor*.

Amy says we can shower if we want to, or we can wait until after the activity. She has a knack for cryptic.

We meet on the lawn twenty minutes later and see a row of army green jerry cans.

"We are going for a walk and will be taking these jerry cans with us," she explains. "They aren't full, but they're heavy enough you won't need another workout today. As you walk, think about what's weighing you down in life. What are the burdens and stresses sapping your energy and eating up your strength?"

"How far are we going?" someone shouts from the back.

"Far enough," Amy replies with a smile. "This will not kill you, trust me." And off she goes, leading the charge, carrying a can herself.

***

We walk for an hour or so. Breaks whenever needed. The trail is mostly empty, but the birds are chatty. We don't talk much after the first few minutes. Having something large and unwieldy to carry, along with the encouragement to think about what weighs us down in life, seems to get the wheels spinning.

I think about the anger I try to hold under the surface. The energy it takes to keep it there. I think of being alone and the question I often ask myself—is it better to be alone forever, or to risk betrayal? I think about loneliness and the rejection I wear like a winter parka—keeping me warm but numbly insulated from the world around me.

I remember how it felt to look for help and find none. I think of the secrets I kept from Mom and Dad and Grandpa and wish I could let them blow away like dandelion seeds. The ache I feel in my arms and shoulders from carrying litres of water is comforting somehow.

No one complains as we walk. The physical act is cathartic. I finally have a way to visualize what I've been doing for years. I've been dragging my pain and sadness and shame everywhere I go. I didn't realize what I'd been doing. I didn't notice how the weight makes me strong in some places but weak and vulnerable in others.

I hear voices in front of me and look up. We have arrived at our destination—a turquoise-blue lake tucked into the forest. David and Katherine and Evan are already there, cooking around a fire. Picnic tables are set with tablecloths and real plates.

We follow Amy to the shore. There's a breeze by the lake, and it tousles my hair with a hello. Amy opens her Bible and reads, "Jesus said to them, 'Come to Me, all who are weary and heavy-laden, and I will give you rest. Take My yoke upon you and learn from

Me, for I am gentle and humble in heart, and you will find rest for your souls. For My yoke is easy and My burden is light.'[109]

"Jesus made this offer to His followers many years ago, and the offer is available for you today," she says. "You don't have to walk through life with these weights and burdens. Jesus is offering you rest. He will take these burdens from you if you will give them up. His arms are wide open to you."

We stand for a few minutes, squinting into the sun. I imagine Jesus standing up to His ankles in the water, hands extended, asking me to come to Him.

"When you're ready to give your burdens to Jesus, simply pour your water into the lake. As you empty the jug, imagine you are releasing your troubles and fears to God." Amy steps aside, and we move closer to the water's edge.

I've heard of Jesus taking my sins to make me clean, but I'd never thought about what else He could take. Does He really want all the stuff I don't know how to handle? Finding a job, forgiving Mom, anger I can't control, my sister Mary's suicide, the shame of being so completely unwanted. I feel so tired. Not from walking a few kilometers carrying a jug of water, but from living years of my life so alone.

I don't want to be alone anymore. I don't want life to stay the way it is. If pouring out these things to Jesus is a way to live a new life, I'm ready for it.

I pick up my jerry can and tip it over until the water gushes out. A sensation of hope wells up inside of me with a gentle tickle similar to a breeze. I'm soaked by the time the last drops are in the lake, but it's appropriate somehow, because I feel refreshed. I look around and see smiles on the faces of my friends. Jason, Connor, Matt, and a few others run to the end of the dock and cannonball into the lake. Guys!

We've all found something to laugh about by the time Katherine calls us to find a seat at the tables.

"You have just surrendered burdens to God, and it is wonderful to live free from what has weighed you down. Letting go is a significant step. What an amazing God we have—one who will gladly take all that is too heavy for us!

"Let us celebrate the way God promises to care for us. There is a loaf of bread on each table." She picks up one of the loaves and holds on to it as she continues. "It's not communion, exactly, but we will break bread together. As we eat, remember Jesus is here with us through Holy Spirit. He called Himself the Bread of Life, and He can nourish and strengthen you today.

"I once read a fascinating account about orphans during WWII. [110] These tiny survivors of incredible suffering were brought to safety in orphanages. Though protected and cared for, the children could not sleep at night. The workers could not understand why.

"After many miserable nights with little sleep, someone had an idea: What if we put the kids to bed at night with a loaf of bread next to them? By giving them something they can touch and smell, they will have hope that tomorrow can also be safe. The bread was a visible reminder of good things to come. It worked wonders.

"As you eat this meal, the bread and eggs and sausages, remember Christ is with you now and always. He offers Himself as the promise of what is to come. You are not alone, and you no longer need to live in fear."

We hold hands around the table and say a blessing. David and Evan bring platters to the table, and does the food ever taste good!

Thursday, 2:02 pm

It felt really nice to jump in the shower and take a nap before meeting again at two. Walking back to the centre without anything to carry was its own lesson on freedom. I gave Connor a piggyback for a few seconds, but he was a very different type of heavy burden.

David has been giving a devotional a few times a day, and we always say the Lord's Prayer together. I don't mind, but this time I notice Jason doesn't pray with us. As soon as we say "Amen," he speaks up.

"David, can I ask why we're doing this again?" Jason sounds annoyed. "What's up with all the repetition? Doesn't God get bored with it? I sure do. I didn't come here to pray meaningless prayers over and over again."

"Jason, I appreciate your honesty." Nothing gets David flustered. "I'm glad you feel safe to say what you're thinking. I wish more people would ask questions like this.

"I studied adult education in grad school and learned some things about learning. When people are trying to master something new—playing squash, speaking German, driving a stick shift, or rocking the saxophone—they understand the necessity of practice, and occasionally, mind-numbing repetition. However, when it comes to spirituality, we are suspicious of anything repetitive or rote or uncomfortable. If we are told to memorize a verse, to sacrifice, to read the Bible every day, or to say the same prayer, we resent it.[111]

"It appears there is something missing in our notion of spiritual growth. There's pushback to the idea of practicing anything. We're terrified of the appearance of earning God's approval, so we throw the baby out with the bathwater.

"Hockey players practice; musicians rehearse; scientists experiment over and over and over again; but we resist the idea that it will take effort to be good at following God. Why is that? What are we afraid of?

"When elite athletes train for important events, they regulate their actions, schedules, diet, speech, thought life, and more. They understand the connection between "normal," "ordinary" actions, and their success. If we paid attention to what shaped our spiritual lives, I think we'd be more picky with our time.

"So, to get back to your question, Jason, we are not saying the Lord's Prayer every day to impress God. We are saying it to get the truth of its words inside us. We can say the words with brains switched off, or we can let the prayer shape us.[112]

"Consider how it begins—*Our Father*. What strikes you about those words in the context of this week? I want to hear from all of you, not only Jason."[113]

"First of all, it's not 'my Father' but 'our Father,'" Rachel says. "We have the same Father."

"Jesus chose a relational word, 'Father,' instead of something formal or authoritarian, like 'Master' or 'Lord,'" Connor says.

"You go to a father when you need help," I say.

"This is good," David says. "Keep going."

"I think it's cool to hear Jesus talking to the Father—it reminds me of all that Trinity stuff—and it shows Jesus knew He wasn't alone… it reminds me I'm not alone, either," Manuel adds.

"I didn't talk to my dad much," Kimmie says, "but I like having someone to call Father."

"Yes, very good," David says again. "Such insight from two words. Well done. Friends, the spiritual life should be lived with this kind of vigor and energy. Why go through life praying in a 'pass the peas' kind of way, when you can turn your heart toward our beloved Father? The difference is night and day.

"Jason, talk to me. What are you thinking now?" David asks.

"I never thought about prayer as practicing something," Jason admits. "It makes sense in that way, but why do we have to say the exact same words? Can't we each say what we want?" he asks.

"Another fabulous question! We could talk about community and participation in something bigger than ourselves, but that conversation will have to wait. In short, there are times it's preferable to improvise in prayer, as Jason suggests, but when we do something together, it's useful to agree on the method."

"Think about it this way," he continues. "How many times have you sung Happy Birthday? Fifty? One hundred? Two hundred? More? Even though it gets boring, we sing it because people know it. We've memorized it. No matter what city you're from or how old you are, you can join in because it's known.

"One of the downsides of our individualism is we can overlook our inclusion in God's global family. [114] Children of divorce are familiar with exclusion and aloneness. Precisely for that reason, it's important we look for ways to stay connected to the larger group. There's nothing more beautiful than saying the Lord's Prayer in a dozen languages with Christians from around the world.

"Jason, I thank you for bringing this topic to the table. However, I'm going to press on and shift our attention to a video clip," David says. He cues a clip of a famous South Korean potter in his workshop. [115] As we watch the video, we're supposed to think about God shaping us, and about our experience of surrender.

I'm mesmerized by the artist and his muddy hands, by what care and attention he gives to what he's shaping. What a mess he makes!

Then I think about what it would be like to completely trust God to shape my life. I find myself resisting the idea of surrender. I've always been stubborn, and I wonder if God gets impatient with me, with how I want things my way and with how I refuse help. Surrender requires absolute trust, and I'm not there.

As a new Christian, I was told faith is a partnership between God and me. It's not either/or; it's both/and. Both of us put effort into the relationship. When I expect God to do everything, I become passive, complacent, and entitled. Maturity comes when I realize my actions and ideas have significance.[116]

The other extreme is to live like God's on a vacation and it's all on me. I push and manipulate. I carry the weight of all my problems. This is a speedy way to get an ulcer.

Somewhere in between is where Christ-followers are supposed to live. God is at work, and we have a part to play. Sometimes our part is to simply give Him permission to do what He wants—then relax and trust Him. Other times, our part is to work relentlessly in pursuit of what's good and right.

I'm not sure where I am on the spectrum. I lean toward thinking I'm on my own. Then I give up when it doesn't work out the way I planned. I forget God is able and willing to help.

The example of the potter and clay only goes so far because the clay has no name, no voice, no emotions, no ability to say yes or no—and this week we've learned these attributes are extremely important to God.

What touches me during the video is how the potter's eyes never stray from the pot he's making. His hands never let go. The tender care of the potter is beautiful. I'd like someone like him shaping my life—someone both tender and qualified.

Chapter Nineteen

The Bible teaches that we are to form attachments with people, not only with God. We are to learn how to feel loved and experience a sense of belonging by being in relationship with others.[117]

Thursday, 7:30 pm

Sloane

We are all sleep-deprived at this point in the week, and Katherine is merciful. Instead of a session, we meet in process groups. For the first time all week, none of the staff are with us. I think they're preparing us to go home and act like adults again.

We're supposed to talk about what we're learning, how we're feeling, and what our experience of the week has been. I feel frustrated because we don't have a leader. What are we trying to accomplish?

Suddenly I realize most of life is like this—groups of people get thrown together, no one tells you what you're supposed to do, and somehow you've got to figure out what you want.

It's cool to hear from the group. It feels easy to laugh and cry with them. They trust me with deep, raw (sometimes ugly) parts of themselves. It's safe to open myself in the same way.

It's after nine when Evan knocks on the door and sits down with us. He wants to hear what we've learned from this experience of community.

I start out, "I told you guys I've been alone a lot, but this week has been different. I only knew a few of you when I got here, but I've felt less alone this week

191

than any other time in my life. I feel like I actually belong. It's amazing." I'll be crying soon if I don't stop.

Connor goes next. "I realize I've been a snob. I've rejected people at church and work... even my roommates. I think, 'he's too old,' 'they're married and I'm single,' 'our personalities are different,' or 'we don't have the same interests,' and stuff like that. I disqualify people from being friends, and that's dumb. Look at us—we're way different, but we got close. I'd trust you guys with anything. I've been looking for the wrong things when it comes to community. I thought people had to be the same, but now I think that's not what matters at all."

"Yeah, I can relate to what Connor is saying," Manuel jumps in. "You could get close and feel connected to just about anybody if they'll listen and be real. So why's it so hard to do that at home? We keep ourselves from the exact thing we want in life."

"It hard because people don't know how to make space for it. I think we have to be the ones to make it happen, you know," Matt says in reply. "At least tell people what we've experienced and show them what genuine community looks like."

"Yeah, people aren't going to spill their guts unless they see us doing it first," Manuel agrees.

Kimmie leans forward and says, "I've noticed it's easier for me to feel close to God when I'm around you guys. Maybe being accepted by you has helped me understand what His love feels like. It's what David said about noticing the connections we have, so we can tune into God's love."

"I've discovered it can be healing to cry," Matt says. "I tried to do without it, but this week I've cried like a banshee, and that's not really my thing. There's this quote Katherine gave us: 'We equate crying with pain. In fact, crying isn't pain; it's the way people release their pain.'[118] It feels good to let go of my pain."

"A takeaway for me is about anger," Manuel offers. "I feel so much anger toward my parents and God. I blamed God because I knew He could handle it, but it's hard to get close to someone I'm angry with. After talking with David, and you, Evan, I realize God feels anger about what happened in my life. And sadness. I don't have to deny my anger. Instead of being angry with God, we can be angry together. I don't want to push God away anymore. I want us to be close again."

"Those are some amazing takeaways," Evan says. The guy has a smile that fills his entire face. "Seriously. You have grown so much this week, and light bulbs have come on. I'm learning from your insights."

Evan prays for us and sends us off to bed—in our own rooms tonight. My pillow is going to feel good.

***

Friday, 6:18 am

I get out of bed early, since I'm not sleeping anyway. It's the last day, and I'm conflicted. I don't want to leave. I've made friends. I fit in. Where else do twenty-two adults have sleepovers and memorial services and do arts and crafts together? Where else do people play the saxophone and wake me up with a guitar concert? Who's gonna make me laugh next week? Who's gonna call me out on my stuff?

I'm going to crash when I get home. Adrenaline can only last so long. How will I control my emotions when I'm alone again? Around this group, my emotions have permission to show up whenever and however they want.

Tears well up, and I dress quickly before my sniffling bothers Rachel. I go for a prayer walk but don't get far before I sit on a rock and cry. I'm not used to so many tears.

**

Friday, 7:40 am

I'm drinking coffee and picking at my food when Amy sits down across from me. My puffy face or lack of eye contact must have tipped her off that all is not well.

"You up for a walk?" she asks, but it's an order more than question.

I stand up, which is easier than speaking, and take the coffee with me.

We walk for a few minutes and find a patch of sunshine to sit in.

"Can you tell me what's going on?" This time it is a question.

She waits while I gather my thoughts.

"I don't know… It's just, we're leaving soon, and I feel more messed up now than when we started. I… I don't know how I'm going to deal with everything when I'm back home."

"I see," she says, picking clover blossoms. "Sloane, it's normal to be sad about leaving your new friends. It's normal to think about what's next. I'm sorry to hear it, though. It's not fun."

"I hate making friends. Nothing but trouble. I should have stayed home."

"Oh, Sloane," Amy says gently, "you probably don't want to hear this, but feeling sad is a really good sign for you."

"Really, it's good for me? Why's that?" I ask. I don't like this feeling-bad-to-be-healthy mumbo-jumbo.

"It's good because it means you've made real connections with people. You've attached—in a healthy way—to the group. Feeling sad is a sign of how deep those connections are. What's good is you chose to let people in... quite a few people, actually. You took steps of vulnerability. You took risks this week, and I'm proud of you."[119] She says it with such an affirming tone that I can't stay angry.

I don't have much practice talking about my feelings. I pick some grass and play with it, watching my fingers turn green. "Okay, I hear you, but it's not just that, Amy. Saying goodbye is the easy part.

"What hope is there for me, seriously?" I continue. "I don't know how to change my life. I can't change my life. It's ruined beyond repair. Me—I've been ruined." My voice breaks. I hate this. "I don't know how to love. I don't trust people. All I see is darkness and loneliness. Even if people say they love me, I don't believe them. It's a disaster." I start crying again, tears from the dark place inside of me. The kind of tears that make me feel worse, not better.

I told myself I was getting by; I was making it work; I could handle whatever came my way. I was totally lying to myself. I've been scraping by, pretending it's all good. To admit things are bad is like announcing I can't handle it.

Why should something as insignificant as my parents splitting up ruin my life? It happens to a million kids a year.[120] I don't want to be the "one in a million" who can't cut it. I'm so pathetic.

"Sloane," Amy says once my tears slow down, "you've made progress this week. I'm impressed by what I've seen in you. But I understand it feels dark."

"Dark, yes, it is dark," I whisper. "It feels hopeless... no matter what I do, I can't change. I can't feel different on the inside. Around and around I go... but it's always the same."

Amy's a good listener. She doesn't fill the space. She never interrupts, which lessens the pressure to talk. She lets me think, and she entertains herself by inspecting the grasses and flowers growing near by.

"I wonder," she begins after an extended silence, "if the trees ever feel the way you do." I raise my eyebrows. She continues, "They contemplate their role in the universe and think, 'My existence is pointless. Consider this—I sprout leaves and blossoms in the spring. The blossoms shrivel, the leaves get big, and fruit ripens in summer. Then the fruit falls off, the leaves fall off, and I sit around, doing nothing, all winter, until it's spring again. What's the purpose of that?'"

"I'd be discouraged if I were a tree," I admit.

"If you have a short-term perspective, it seems a waste of time," she agrees. "Where's the progress? It seems like a lot of wasted effort. But if you know the big picture, it's another story. Every year the tree is changed. Each year it becomes stronger. Its roots burrow deeper; its branches extend wider and higher." She leans back to pat the tree beside us. "Each year the tree increases its capacity to provide shade and to produce fruit... which is nice for us. Birds build homes and bees gather pollen... which is nice for them. It's the same tree—same roots and trunk—but it becomes stronger and more mature. It grows up into what it's meant to be."

I remember watering a tree in our front yard as a kid. The tree and I were the same height when we planted it. Last year, on the pilgrimage to our childhood home, it towered over me.

"Sloane, everyone who has ever wanted to grow and change experiences exactly what you describe; a frustration with the way things are, a desire for something different, even despair over how long it takes. Those emotions are part of the journey. Without them, you would never move beyond where you are."

She's making sense. Frustration always builds up until it pushes me to do something.

"I wish all that stuff with your family had never happened. It was wrong that your parents broke their word. It's a tragedy that you grew up without a stable home. I can't change that... even though I'd really like to. We don't get to erase the painful parts of our story, but there are people who see you for who you are, people who would never think the divorce is a reflection of your value. There are people who love you and will continue to love you. There are people you can count on."

I want to nod, to show her I've got it together, but I don't see the point. I could nod until my head falls off and never feel different.

Amy leans back on the tree and keeps going. "My sister and her husband adopted a baby boy a few years ago. The reasons his mom gave him up are complicated... tragic. One day he will find out what happened, and he will have to deal with his past. He will walk through the agony of abandonment and rejection." Amy turns to look at me, and I see tears in her eyes. "I hate even thinking about it! My sister and brother-in-law are preparing for it... and the kid's only three! What they tell him will break his heart. He will be angry. He'll push them away. I'm not looking forward to that phone call.

"But for now, my sister and her husband do everything they can to show him and tell him he's wanted and valuable. His birth-mom's decision has no relevance on how lovable he is."

"Yeah, I get that," I say. And I do. It's easy to relate to the pain of being rejected by your mother.

"Nothing can erase that part of his story," she continues. "There's no way to erase parts of your story either, my friend. But I have the same hope for my nephew as I do for you—the comfort of God's love and deep connection to those around you."[121]

Being compared to a small child helps somehow, makes it simple. Like Amy, I want her nephew to bypass the coming pain, but I know denial won't help. Being showered by a waterfall of parental love and acceptance is a good plan, a preemptive strike. What other hope is there? What but love can displace rejection?

Maybe there's a way God can do that in my life. Maybe His love and hope can drive out the pain and fear trapped inside.[122]

I feel a bit better. And hungry. It's been an intense morning, and it's not even nine. I thank Amy, and we walk back. There's something I need to talk with Katherine about.

***

One of the first things you should teach people is that they can trust the growth process, no matter how they feel in the midst of it. It is not going to be only up to them to "make it." The Holy Spirit is always going to be there, drawing them to God and to greater and greater growth.[123]

Chapter Twenty

It is not enough to convince our intellects; our imaginations need to be caught by—and caught up into—the Story of God's restorative, reconciling grace for all of creation. It won't be enough for us to be convinced; we need to be moved.[124]

Friday, 9:01 am

Sloane

Day Five: Being Part of Something Glorious

The kitchen staff is helpful but confused by my list of items. The talk with Amy reminded me of something I saw once at youth group. Katherine said my idea would be an appropriate introduction for the morning.

I carry my equipment to the front: empty water glass, pitcher of water, random collection of condiments, large basin.

My delivery won't be polished, but they'll get the point. I fill the glass halfway with water. "This glass represents a life, your life, my life—beautiful and clear," I explain. "Time goes by, and things get messy." I slowly add mustard, soy sauce, hot sauce, vinegar, and BBQ sauce as I talk. "Parents leave, someone hurts you, cruel words are said." The water becomes dark and smells funky. "You are alone and afraid... suddenly you can't see anything. You are lost."

I hold up the glass for everyone to see. "When this is your life, it's easy to feel hopeless. What hope is there for you? For us? What are we to do?" I ask.

I hold the glass over the basin, take the pitcher, and slowly add water to the glass. "Imagine this water represents God's presence and truth in our lives." The clean water begins to dilute the murky. "God is not afraid to come into our messiness... that's what we learn from Jesus. God pays attention to us. He remembers who we are. He knows what we have been created for. He can change us."

The glass is about to overflow, and I hesitate.

"Keep it coming, Sloane!" Connor shouts from the back. So I do.

The dirty water spills over the glass and onto my hand. So much junk comes out! I pour slowly. Change takes time. God's love changes how we feel. He restores. The container doesn't change, but we're changed on the inside.

I pour all the water into the glass. I'd been so enthusiastic with the demo that the remaining water is still cloudy. A flaw in my design. "Well, um, you guys get the idea, right?" I stumble. "If I had more water, the glass would get really clear." I look pleadingly at Katherine.

Rachel jumps up front with her water bottle in hand and pours it into the glass. I wasn't expecting that. Manuel comes next and does the same. Soon it's a stampede. Everyone wants in on the action. I laugh at their enthusiasm. Every water bottle in the room is emptied, and the point is well made.

I feel Katherine's arm on my shoulder. "That was absolutely perfect, Sloane," she says. I smile at her and take my seat with the group. I need a towel.

"Today we will talk about the story we are part of. Sloane's illustration is a beautiful picture of this. Life is about knowing God and reflecting Him to the world. He invites us to join His restoration plan on earth.[125] Sloane's example touched on the three key ideas for today."

She writes on the board:
Creation
The Fall
Redemption

"God created people in His image, to live in relationship with Father, Son, and Spirit, to be part of something glorious. They are the perfect relationship, and they want to share that love with us.

"But something destructive happened and continues to happen—we choose self over God. We choose foolishness over love. We forget what life is about… perhaps we never knew. We reject perfect love. The Fall disrupted humanity's connection with God on a global scale and on the personal level. I think you know what I'm talking about.

"From the Fall onward, our understanding is distorted and clouded: by our choices, by the actions of others, by the circumstances of life. Like the glass of water, we become dark, polluted, confused, and hopeless. But God is not confused.

"The final act of His story is Redemption. God is at work now, in my life, in your life, on earth, to restore creation to His original intent—relationship with Him and freedom to love.[126]

"Watching you pour water into Sloane's glass was a poignant image of restoration. I'm glad Sloane didn't have two jugs of water. If she'd had more water, we would have sat and watched. Instead, we were moved by what we saw, and the natural response was to get up and join her."

"My friends, we are part of a very big, very important story. We are invited to participate. Until you understand this, you will stay in your chair, watching what others do, bemoaning the state of the world. Eventually you will stop caring or get bitter.

"Restoration is our calling. It's our destiny. I have seen you in action this week and noticed the way you've loved each other. What happened here will stick with you for life. God has been at work, through you, to restore one another. It is not insignificant."

I zone out a bit, the first time all week. What she's saying reminds me of my talk with Connor at the campsite. Was that just six days ago?

Doing God's work is something I've heard about since I became a believer. Each sermon and exhortation to "change the world" only reminds me how I'm letting God down. It's way too big a job, and there's no way I can succeed.

It never occurred to me I'm supposed to do God's work with others. I'm used to being alone and self-sufficient. I assumed it's more spiritual to be alone. But something clicked this morning when Rachel and Manuel and Connor joined me at the front. I felt so happy. I felt happier in those moments than I can remember feeling in a long time. I envisioned doing significant things together. If I've learned anything this week, it's the value of connection. God's never been alone, so why would He expect me to be alone?[127]

I tune back in, and Katherine's talking about finding our place in God. Some people think because God is huge and we are small, we automatically disappear into Him. She gets worked up talking about this, and I see the saxophone-playing artist come to life. "No!" she declares. "We don't disappear into God. We don't lose ourselves in Him; we find our rightful place. He made us unique, and He wants us to stay that way! I will never stop being Katherine. But now I am Katherine-in-God, I am Katherine-as-part-of-His-body. Connection to Him is changing me."

I'm glad to hear this. I want my voice and my ideas to matter. I want to have a place. I don't want to be lost in the crowd, even if it's a good crowd. I don't want to get swallowed up and disappear. I've spent too many years invisible.

Katherine continues, "The body of Christ is not a blob of sameness, but a tapestry of distinct threads. You are a distinct thread, and you are connected to the rest of us. We need you. We need all the parts. You have something to give us, and there's no shame in receiving from the rest of us."

She talks about the family of God. This always trips me up, because family is not a positive word for me. In fact, it represents so much of what I resent, detest, and avoid. It's a word I prefer to spit out. But maybe God can clear out the junk clouding my view of family and make it fresh again.

Family is not always custody fights and rejection and conflict. It's home, belonging, and being together. You're supposed to learn belonging from family, but I didn't. I want to belong to something. Or someone. Maybe both. I want to know a connection that's permanent.[128]

In God's family, I am chosen and wanted. My identity as His child overwrites all other descriptors—rejected, single, tainted by my miserable family. There's no pecking order in God's family. I have the same rights and position as every other kid. There's one family, and I'm part of it![129]

It's comforting to know I'm part of God's family, but uncomfortable too. There's safety when you're on the inside, but I'm terrified to be part of something I can't escape.

I tune in as Katherine explains how children of divorce struggle to piece together the story of their life and family. The narrative is confused, and details are mixed up. The family timeline has been chopped, and we aren't sure where that leaves us.[130] I can relate to that. My life feels like a 500-piece puzzle that's missing a hundred pieces.

Many times I've felt disconnected and unattached—a helium balloon drifting into the sky. I've felt like a kite with no one holding the string. I don't want to feel this way. I want God to be my anchor. I want Him to bring security to my insecure heart.

I know it's not magic. There's no special prayer to change everything. I have to grow into my identity as His child. I have to build my emotional memory until I'm sure His promises are trustworthy. It sounds like so much work.

I remember Amy's lamenting trees. I want to embrace the value of growing leaves and shedding leaves and waiting for winter to pass. I want to trust the process of growth and change.

I'm at a crossroads of sorts. Will I trust God to lead me to the good places He promises? Will I surrender my independence to Him? Will I accept help that comes my way? I'm afraid, but nothing else has worked. All my strategies to avoid pain have failed miserably.

I need a nap.

***

I go through coffee break in a daze. If I talk to anyone, they'll ask questions I don't know how to answer. Sometimes a woman needs her space.

Katherine puts us into discussion groups to talk about ways God has helped us to see Him or ourselves more clearly.

The glass of water example made it seem easy, but the consensus in my group is that clarity does not appear on demand. Revelation can be welcomed, but not produced. Kimmie feels refreshed during worship at church. For her, the words of the songs are like water from the pitcher, making things clearer. Jason remembers breakfast with a mentor, when his value to God seemed crystal-clear. For me, there was one time over a sinkful of dishes I first accepted the idea that God had made me on purpose. I felt loved and wanted. Evan was reading the Bible on the bus when God's hope and joy felt more real than ever before.

All these stories are told reverently, but a bit sheepishly too. The circumstances were normal, ordinary, and the impact was hard to put into words, yet undeniable. We did things we normally do, but that particular time, they became extraordinary. There was no rhyme or reason to it. Why did God show up when I was washing dishes that day? Why are most days unremarkable?

The conversation gives me another thing to contemplate. What can I do to hear God more? How do I pay attention to what He's doing? When do I give Him time to speak? The noise of my iPod and apps and YouTube must make it hard for Him to get a word in edgewise.

There's something to be said for making space for God to speak. This week, I discovered that if I'm willing to have the conversation—about pain or loss or frustration—I usually get some answers. Not complete answers that make everything fit, and not always the answer I want to hear, but new perspective on why or how. An awareness of how far I've come. Deep fellowship with people who understand.

At the campsite, Connor talked about pointing himself in the direction of Jesus, trying to move forward, even though he can't tell exactly where he's headed. I want to move forward too. Staying here isn't fun. I want to keep my focus on Jesus.

The next assignment is to meditate on the parable of the prodigal son. We are supposed to read the story and imagine we are in it. What can we see, smell, and hear? What emotions do we feel? What thoughts come to mind? What might God want to say through the story?

I find a spot on the grass and stretch out. I read the familiar passage.[131] My imagination's pretty good. Quickly I'm in the story, imagining all that's happened since I took my inheritance and ran away to the big city:

> I'm such an idiot! Why did I leave in the first place? Things weren't that bad at home. I was determined to prove I was someone important. Trying to be big-spender-party-girl with amazing clothes. It was awesome while it lasted. I always knew people were flocking to me for what they could get.

> And look at me now… greasy hair, stained clothes, cracked and dirty nails. My breath smells. Every part of me smells. Shame makes my head sink. I have no one to turn to. All my friends were fakes.

> The humiliation is thick. Every step is like dragging through mud. The world is laughing at me, crossing its arms in scorn, ready to spit in my direction. I have nowhere to turn. Everyone I leaned on is long gone. My money is gone. I'm an idiot.

> I walk in the direction that will eventually take me home. The road is dusty. The grit makes

my eyes water. I don't know what I want—to reach the front door, or to stay away. I have nothing to offer, nothing to bargain with, nothing to impress anyone.

I think about what I'll say. Please tell Mr. Kovalchuck there is a woman here asking for a job as a maid. No, I don't want to see him. I'd prefer if he didn't see me. Please let me sneak in the side door.

They will recognize me in a second. I wish there were a way to stay anonymous and die in my shame. The idea of hurting him again makes me cringe. But I can't think of anywhere else to go.

It's getting dark and hard to see. Should I stop for the night? I don't have a blanket or coat. I keep moving. It's warmer when I walk.

I become aware that someone is beside me. Not close enough to touch, but present. I keep my head down and see the feet and legs of a man walking next to me. What if he recognizes me? I don't want anyone to see how bad I look.

The light is weak, and I wonder how much he can see. Why would someone be on this street at dusk? Why doesn't he speak? I'm not afraid to be on an empty road with a stranger. I'm near home, and I feel safe.

My curiosity gets the better of me. I look up. I see my father's eyes looking back. I'm shocked. He's not. All this time, he knew it was me.

"Sloane," he says. There's such tenderness in it that his voice is almost a whisper.

I stop walking, and he stops.

"Daddy?" I say, with a question in my voice. What will he say?

"You've finally come home." I feel his arms around me. I collapse into him. If he were to let go, I'd crumple to the ground. "This is the very best day!" he says and I feel him shake with laughter and tears.

...And then I'm back on the grass. The sensation of His arms around me is fresh in my mind. It was wonderful to be wrapped in His embrace, not afraid of anything. He'd forgiven me. I mattered to Him. He'd been waiting for me since the day I left, walking the road each night in the hope I'd come back.

I matter to God. God sees me—not the imaginary Sloane in that parable, but the real Sloane lying on the grass in Banff. He waited a long time for me. Years and years. He endured my angry outbursts, my mockery, all the times I cursed Him.

He cried over me when I refused to cry for myself. He waited for me so patiently, whispering love in my ear, hoping I would hear it one day. He never gave up. Every day He spends with me is the happiest day of His life. How can it get better than living with your beloved?

I think of my favorite verses in Ephesians. I flip to the page and copy these words into my journal:

...And I pray that you, being rooted and established in love, may have power, together with all the saints, to grasp how wide and long and high and deep is the love of Christ, and to know this love that surpasses knowledge—that you may be filled to the measure of all the fullness of God. Ephesians 3:17-19

I roll onto my back. "Father," I say aloud, "please help me grasp this!"

Chapter Twenty-One

Friday, 6:27 pm

Sloane

When we get to our room after canoeing, there are elegant invitations waiting for Rachel and me. There's a bouquet of flowers on the desk and a bottle of sparking apple juice. Our tailored outfits from Isabel's shop are hanging in the closet. It's possible Rachel and I let out a few undignified squeals.

We put on our fancy dresses, and there are no mishaps as we do our hair and get ready. It's much different than preparing for the memorial service a few nights ago.

"So this is it," Rachel says. I see tears in her eyes.

"Yeah, but it's not over yet," I offer.

"Tomorrow night, I'll be back home, and I'll probably never see you again." Her tears escape.

A week ago I would have told her not to cry—of course we'll see each other again, and besides, it's not a big deal. But now I know better. I don't say anything. I reach for her arm and give it a squeeze.

"I'm not used to being loved like this," she continues, "and it's going to be brutal to go back home again. It would have been easier if you'd all been horrible!"

We laugh at that.

"I know what you mean," I say and decide to risk sharing my own feelings. "Being here is the first time I've really felt like I belong in any group." If I'm not careful I'll cry too, and I've already cried a lot today.

"Sloane, I'm happy I came anyway," Rachel says. "At least I know what I'm aiming for now.

Healthy relationships are possible. Can you believe I've been around these great guys all week and don't have a crush on any of them? That's a first." She laughs. "Not that I would be opposed to future possibilities…"

"Where do I sign up?" I tease.

"I wonder how other people live without these kinds of friendships. I mean, we're not the only ones who feel like outsiders most of the time, are we?"

"That's a good question. In this I think we're pretty normal," I suggest. "It seems everybody wants connection, and us kids of divorce have some extra catching up to do."

I get the Kleenex box from the bathroom and hand it to Rachel. "I was thinking about that body of Christ stuff Katherine mentioned today—you know, how we are one body, one family… we're supposed to look out for each other."

"Yeah, it sounded fantastic."

"What would it look like if we actually did that stuff?" I ask. "Not a token 'God's peace, sister' at church, but paying attention to each other, choosing to be in each other's lives, keeping the conversations of this week going."

"You want me to move to Saskatoon?" she says in mock horror.

"Where's the love?" I pretend to be offended. "I could move to Vancouver… are there any good jobs there?" I laugh for the first time about not having a job. "Does connection have to depend on geography? I mean, could we still be in each other's lives a distance?"

"Hmm," Rachel chews her lip, which is her thinking face. "Connection isn't always based on geography, but 'outta sight, outta mind' is true a lot of the time."

"Maybe it's crazy to say this, very Junior High camp of me, but I'd like to stay in touch once we go home. You're the kind of friend I don't want to give up easily."

"Thanks for saying that, Sloane." She gets up and gives me a hug. "You're easy to love, you know?"

I don't know. I'm not sure what to say.

I hug her back and clear my throat. "We can talk more about it later tonight," I suggest. "Shall we go to this fancy-schmancy banquet?"

"Most definitely! Banquet-away!... Just give me a minute to fix my makeup."

***

Friday, 7:06 pm

When we get to the dining room, all the tables are arranged into one huge table, and it looks like Martha Stewart was in charge of décor. Will the Queen arrive in a few minutes?

There's an overtone of joy in the room. Everyone smiles. Everyone looks good, happy, relaxed. I feel comfortable myself, which is odd, since I'm wearing heels. Then I realize what feels so good is *belonging*.

Our seats are assigned, and I find myself sitting between Connor and Rachel. Someone's been paying attention to who's friends with who, though there's no one in the group I wouldn't want to sit beside.

There are three stations set up in various corners of the room. David explains that they represent Father, Son, and Spirit. For Father, there is a potter's wheel—authentic, with mud and splatters, drop cloth, tools for shaping clay, and a few pots in various stages of completion. For Son, there is a rough cross, probably made out of trees from the yard. It's draped with a purple cloth. For Spirit, there's an image of flickering

213

flames projected on the screen. It fills the room with a warm glow, as captivating as a real campfire.

We stand in our places, and a staff member reads a poem (maybe it's a prayer) from each of the three corners, talking about the beauty and love and connection of our Triune God.

The visuals remind us we are not alone. We have been invited in by God and included in the Trinity's love for each other. We belong at God's table. We are in His family, with all the privileges of sonship and daughterhood. David prays for us to be able to tune in more to the love and truth of God and that in Him we will find acceptance and security.

We sit down, and I can't stop smiling. Everyone is smiling.

The meal is delicious. Normally I'm a utilitarian eater, living on granola bars and apples, but I can appreciate a gourmet meal when it's staring me in the face. Just when I think the meal is done, the plates are whisked away, and another course appears, as if out of thin air.

I lose track of what course we're on, and all of a sudden I think about how much this week cost and how I didn't pay my own way. Someone else footed the bill.

I need to get away for a few minutes. I get up and head for the bathroom.

I push open the door and see Katherine at the sink. "Hi, Sloane. You look lovely," she says.

"Thanks. You do, too," I say automatically.

"But you don't look quite so happy," she says slowly, taking in the expression on my face and my posture. "Do you want to tell me about it?" She gestures to the chairs beside the mirrors.

Must I melt down in the middle of the banquet? Couldn't I pick a better time? I sigh, then take a deep breath and say, "Someone paid my way to the retreat, and it occurs to me I don't really belong here. I feel like a charity case, an imposter."

"I see," Katherine says in reply.

"I had almost fooled myself into thinking I belonged here. In truth, I'm on the outside, looking in, as always," I say, and the tears begin.

She lets me cry for a bit, patting me on the arm. "What I hear you say is that belonging is based on earning your place; is that right?" she asks.

"Something like that." I dab the Kleenex at my tears, trying to avoid raccoon eyes. "I want to hold my head up high, you know, without the shame of sneaking in on a scholarship."

"Right, because scholarship implies some degree of shame, and if you were given a scholarship, it can always be taken back."

"Yep. What's been given can always be un-given. Only count on what you earn yourself."

We sit there for a while. "I see your logic, Sloane," she says. "But would you be willing to hear another perspective on it?" she asks.

"Sure. Why not?" I reply flatly.

"Citizenship in the ancient Roman Empire was a very good thing to have. It granted rights and freedoms everyone wanted. To be born a Roman put you on a fast track to success. However, if you didn't comply with your family's wishes, you could be disowned. When that happened, you lost everything you'd had: title, status, property, freedom. The threat of what they could lose kept people in line."

"Okay…?" I say. Where is she going with this?

"On the other hand, if someone were adopted into a Roman family, brought in from the outside, the law was different. Once adopted, there was no way to be disowned. It was a forever thing. Parents could not change their minds or cancel the adoption."[132]

"Yeah… but what does it have to do with me?" I ask.

"Sloane, when Paul writes to the believers in Ephesus, which was a colony of Rome, he tells them faith in God is like being adopted into His family.[133] Born into pagan families, these men and women had only recently become Christians. They grew up worshiping the god Artemis. They were as far from Jewish as possible. Jesus was unlike any other god they'd known. When they responded to His invitation, they entered a family that never dissolves.

"When you said 'yes' to following God, you were adopted into His family. You have the same rights and privileges as every member of the family. It's not a tier system.

"So what if you didn't pay for the retreat? Big deal. Maybe God wants to make a point with this extravagant gift. Maybe He's trying to demonstrate that you don't have to do it on your own. He is the kind of father who takes care of His daughter.

"Instead of viewing it as a mark against you, what if you saw this week as a special gift from God? You won the jackpot, my friend! You are the object of His delight."

"I never thought about it that way before," I admit. "I'm not very good at receiving from people."

"Well, it's not too late to learn." She smiles, and I smile back. "What do you think? Are you ready to get back to the party and enjoy what our Father is giving us?"

"Yes, I think I am," I say. I grab another Kleenex from the box and stand up.

***

The dishes are cleared when we get back. Dessert is coming later, but we'll digest a bit before stuffing ourselves again. Katherine had asked each of us to prepare something to share with the group.

We go around the table, each of us standing in place to address the group. When it's my turn I open my Bible to Psalm 126 and read the whole thing.

> "It seemed like a dream, too good to be true,
> When God returned Zion's exiles.
> We laughed, we sang,
> We couldn't believe our good fortune.
> We were the talk of the nations—
> 'God was wonderful to them!'
> God *was* wonderful to us;
> We are one happy people.
>
> "And now, God, do it again—
> Bring rains to our drought-stricken lives
> So those who planted their crops in despair
> Will shout hurrahs at the harvest,
> So those who went off with heavy hearts
> Will come home laughing, with armloads of blessing."[134]

When I've finished reading, I say, "I was thinking about the concept of 'already but not yet' that Katherine explained earlier this week. That phrase perfectly describes my life. In some ways, I've experienced the joy and good fortune this psalm talks about. My life is different since I met Jesus—and I'm grateful. But in other ways, I'm intensely aware that I need His help. My life feels drought-stricken, dry, and lifeless right now. I need God to 'do it again.' I want to believe there are good things ahead. I want to find my

217

home in Him and to be so full of His love I come home laughing."

I sit down and listen to the others around the table. Each voice so precious. Each friend so courageous. Each person known and loved a little more than at the start of the week.

I think of the people I love who aren't at the table: my brother Andrew; my dad. In my mind's eye, I imagine the banquet table growing longer, stretching out through the open doors to the patio outside. The table climbs over the mountain peaks and through the valleys, beside the blue-green lakes of the Rocky Mountains, across the prairies and wheat fields to my home in Saskatchewan. I see a table of connection and belonging spreading around the world, proclaiming to every broken heart, "There's a place here for you. You are wanted. You are loved. You belong with us. Leave your life of fear and loneliness behind, and come to God's table."

***

Saturday, 1:38 am

I'm lying in bed. It's so quiet I can hear my watch ticking on the bedside table. It was hard to say good night to everyone, but the practical ones leaving early began the migration, and the rest of us went along. Time to bite the bullet.

Rachel and I talked more about staying connected. We came up with a list of accountability questions and agreed to email the answers to each other every Sunday.[135] I like the idea of someone checking up on me, someone who expects to hear from me each week. I realize most of my friendships are hit or miss—

we hang out if it works, but it gives the impression that I'm a low priority.

Amy said goodbyes are sad when people matter to you, because you've let them in, and I have. I let Rachel and Amy and Connor and others in. At least they don't all live far away.

Rachel and I decided to take control of our friendship. We didn't choose our family, but we can choose our friends. I don't know how long it will last, our email pact, but I look forward to practicing commitment.

If I had to explain what I learned this week, I'd talk about the connection between the inner world and the outer world.

What you think about shapes you. Every time you walked through the front door at Mom's house or Dad's house, you were reminded you're not wanted (they chose someone else, not you). No matter which house you're in, you intrude on a life that's not yours. You don't fully belong; you're a part-time participant.

What you experienced sticks with you. It gets inside of you. Names you're called (step-daughter). Habits you learned (packing and unpacking). What you say (it doesn't matter, see you next year). The family you have (I love you kids, but I can't live with you anymore).

Repetition leaves a mark on you just like the books you read, the songs you know, the TV you watch. A diet of anger and bitterness and rejection breeds more of the same, until you can't imagine anything else.

Being human means being shaped by what you think and do and experience. This can be a good thing or a bad thing, but it's a real thing. Ignoring it doesn't help.

I see there's a battle between what I've experienced and the life God wants for me. My mom abandoned me, but God chose me. I grew up feeling alone, but God is always with me. I see myself as an outsider, but God has brought me in. I'm wanted. I'm accepted.

Which things will I allow to shape me? Which way of life will I pursue—one of isolation, or one of connection? Will I let God work in me, or will I hold Him at arm's length?

Being vulnerable is risky. It's scary. But without vulnerability, how will things ever turn around?

God's working, and I have to work too. God gives me a say in this shaping. He lets me choose what to dwell on, what to feed on.

Holy Spirit is at work—leading me, encouraging me, whispering in my ear, singing hope over me. I'm not alone, and I don't have to figure it out on my own.

I want to hear the song He sings over me. I want to hear His voice… through beauty, through friends, through the words of my family's ancient prayers.

Father, please keep teaching me. Please keep shaping me. I want to experience Your life. I want to know I'm Yours. I want to leave the life of aloneness and join Your life of continual connection and belonging.

I think of these things, and I fall asleep.

***

The community of the church cannot eliminate the deep… fractures that occur when divorce strikes, but it can, in its communal life, stand with and for these children, bearing their brokenness. In this way it can hold them together, by whispering in words and deeds, "Your pain is beyond comprehension, and you suffer, but know that we share your suffering. You are not alone. You may have lost the union in the community that created you, but you are secure in this community that knows a power that brings life out of death, a power in which isolation gives way to belonging."[136]

"Do not let your heart be troubled; believe in God, believe also in Me. In My Father's house are many dwelling places; if it were not so, I would have told you; for I go to prepare a place for you. If I go and prepare a place for you, I will come again and receive you to Myself, that where I am, there you may be also.[137]

"I've loved you the way My Father has loved Me. Make yourselves at home in My love."[138]

A Final Word from the Author

Dear friend,

You have made it to the end of this story. I hope you're glad you stayed with me the whole way. You may be wondering, *What's next for me or those I love?* Perhaps you feel stirred up, a bit confused, partially hopeful and partially discouraged. You may be inspired to do something to change, or you may want to climb in bed and pull the covers over your head. Perhaps you can identify with the journey of Sloane and the others, or perhaps your journey is quite different from what you've read in these pages.

As you've heard the characters in the story say, there is no *fix* or *solution* to being a child of divorce. This experience will always be part of your story. However, the way you embrace it and walk with it can make a big difference in your relationships, inner world, emotional health, and your future.

So, if you are wondering, *What do I do now?* Here are a few things to consider:

- Taking the time to read this book and look at your life is a big step! Treat yourself to coffee, ice cream, pie, a walk around the lake, or whatever you do when you want to celebrate!
- Who in your life could you talk with about the experience of your parents' divorce? There are many people out there who would listen well. Maybe you even know someone else who could benefit from sharing their story. Can you contact a friend and arrange a coffee date to talk specifically about what each of you has been through?

- Is now the time to meet with a counselor? I avoided counseling for years, intimidated by what it would be like and afraid of the stigma attached to it. But after the first few sessions, I wished I'd started ten years earlier!*
- If you haven't worked through the **activity and application** section at the end of the book, you may want to do so in the coming days and weeks. Other readers have found these questions helpful as they consider the impact of divorce on their lives.
- If you would like to learn more about how divorce has impacted others, I have listed many resources in the endnotes. You may want to read a couple of these books. *Generation Ex* was the first book I read about adult children of divorce, and I still refer to it. A few other non-fiction books on the top of my list are: *Between Two Worlds*, *The Unexpected Legacy of Divorce,* and *The Children of Divorce.*
- You may want to see if there are any support groups for ACOD in your church or city. I haven't found one near me but would love to hear about what is out there. A place to start would be a google search of "DivorceCare" and "DivorceCare4Kids."

A tendency many of us have is to pull back, hunker down, and tell ourselves we don't need help or healing. Since we've made it this far already, why change? The quote "If we do what we've always done, we'll get what we've always got" challenges my thinking and motivates me to look for ways to alter my habits of thinking and interaction. Instead of withdrawal, I'm practicing asking for help. Instead of isolation, I'm looking for ways to be involved with others. Instead of pretending everything is fine, I'm confessing to friends (and the occasional stranger) that my parents' divorce has impacted me in more ways than I realized. I want to learn better ways of relating to others.

Take courage, my friend—you have come this far, and you've done an amazing job! You have a depth of strength, love, and guts that is astonishing. The benefits of being known and seen for your true self are worth the effort and risk to get you there.

My prayer is for you to discover new and life-giving ways of relating to yourself and others. I pray you will be able to acknowledge and grieve what you have lost, that you will develop a deep sense of connection to God, and that you will find a place of belonging in community. I pray you will learn how to share authentically and listen to others as they do the same. The antidote (so to speak) to loneliness is knowing others and being known—and that is something everyone longs for, and we all are in the process of learning to do better.

I have created a dedicated email for those who have read *Come Home Laughing* and want to share their experience or send me a message. I can be reached at: comehomelaughing@gmail.com.

With hope and blessing,
Tanya

*Finding a counselor and paying for sessions may seem like huge obstacles to overcome. If this is the case for you, consider asking your pastor for suggestions (or connecting to a local church, if you haven't yet, and approaching the pastor about this). Many churches have a network of counselors and psychologists and could give you some recommendations. Also, many churches are willing to subsidise the cost of counseling sessions.

Application and Reflection Activities

Reading a book about divorce can stir up many thoughts, ideas, and questions. You may have the desire to think, process, or talk about what you are reading and learning. These questions can get you started. Feel free to answer as few or as many as you'd like, and in whatever order you'd like. You may want to simply think about them, or you may want to journal, write, draw, or talk with someone about them.

Chapter 1

1. Have you ever read a book about divorce or adult children of divorce? What are some of your expectations of reading this book?
2. Are you more comfortable initiating relationships or waiting for others to approach you?
3. Which of your friends are adult children of divorce? How often do you talk about your childhood and the divorce? Would you like to talk about it more with them? How could you bring up the conversation in a way that could benefit both of you?
4. Are you aware of events, people, experiences, or places that trigger you? What are they? What do you notice about yourself when you are in these situations?

Chapter 2

1. Would you say you are someone who generally avoids relational conflict, or someone who fights and pushes when you want something to change? Where do you

think you learned this style of relating? How effective is it in dealing with relational challenges in your life?

2. Think about someone in your life who is a good listener. What does it feel like to know that this person will give of their time and effort to hear what you want to say?

3. Consider answering some or all of the questions that were asked at the panel discussion:

    a. How old were you at the time of your parents' divorce?

    b. What reason were you given for the divorce?

    c. What do you remember about life before the divorce?

    d. How do you think the divorce has shaped your view of love and relationships?

    e. How would you say your parents' divorce impacted you on a personal level?

    f. What would you like people to know about divorce?

    g. Can you identify a turning point that helped you deal with the divorce?

    h. What's your relationship like with your parents now?

If you think it would be helpful for you to discuss some of the answers to these questions with a friend, with whom could you do this?

Chapter 3

1. How comfortable are you asking others for help? Would you rather give help to someone, or receive help? Why do you think that is?
2. How comfortable are you being vulnerable with your friends?
3. When's the last time you chose to be vulnerable with someone when you could have hidden instead? How did it go? What happened? Was the result positive or negative? Did your experience make you more or less likely to be vulnerable in the future?

Chapter 4

1. At different times in the story, Sloane considers her friendships and where she feels connection. Draw a "map" of the relationships in your life and how they connect to each other and to you. Think about the places and ways you find connection and community. Are there any changes you'd like to see in your life?
2. How would you describe your skills as a listener? How patient/comfortable are you in being willing to let people express emotions— even the negative ones? Can you identify with any of the *dos* or *don'ts* from the article Sal sent to Sloane? Which ones?
3. Sloane talks about things that changed for her family after her Mom left—not dressing up for Halloween, laundry and pigtails not looking the same. What are some of the things that changed for you and your family after the divorce?

Chapter 5

1. What are some songs, poems, or videos that are a source of comfort or encouragement to you at the moment? What do you like about what they communicate?
2. List some of the unspoken messages you learned as a child regarding your parents. (Examples of unspoken messages: Mom doesn't care enough about me to defend me. Dad always chooses work over me. Mom is more interested in her other kids than she is in me. Dad wants to be with his new wife more than he wants to be with me.)

Chapter 6

1. Sal connects emotional memory with events that help you to remember and experience a person's love for you, even when that person is not present. What are some significant experiences that have shaped your emotional memory as it relates to God or other important relationships?
2. Generally, how aware would you say you are of your emotional state? (Rate on a scale of 1-5.)

> 1 - Not at all. I have emotions?
> 2 - A little bit. Emotions don't play a big role in my life.
> 3 - Moderately. I'm learning to identify my emotional state.
> 4 - Quite aware. Sometimes they catch me by surprise, but I usually know how I'm feeling.

5 - Extremely. I am very aware of my emotions and their role in my daily life.

What do you do when you feel emotions you don't want to feel?

3. How comfortable are you in expressing your emotions in a healthy way? (Rate on a scale of 1-5.)

1 - Not comfortable at all. I don't see a need to express emotions.

2 - Uncomfortable. There are rare occasions when emotions need to be expressed.

3 - Moderately comfortable. I'm willing to express emotions in the right circumstances.

4 - Comfortable. I am able to express a range of emotions in most settings.

5 - Very comfortable. I know when and how to express my feelings in helpful and healthy ways.

Chapter 7

1. Sal's professor says attachment is the deep desire we have to connect with others. Think about people you have connected with deeply over the course of your life (childhood, teen years, and adulthood). What do you notice about how you attach to others? List some of the healthy and unhealthy ways you attach to others.

2. In this chapter Sloane talks with Jake's mom about forgiveness. Would you say you're someone who finds it easy to forgive, or someone who tends to hold grudges? How can

you tell it's the right time for you to forgive someone?

3. Do you have anyone in your life in the role of a mentor or coach? Someone wise you can go to with your hard questions? Perhaps now is the time to look for someone you could ask to meet with you in this capacity. Write down the names of some possible people.

Chapter 8

1. Spend some time journaling about the topic of vulnerability. What are some of the risks of being vulnerable? What are some benefits of being vulnerable?

2. In this chapter, Roger makes some statements about how he views children of divorce. Have you had people downplay how much divorce impacted you? What other things have people said to you about children of divorce?

3. What would you say are some of the drawbacks and some of the benefits you have experienced as a child of divorce?

4. In this chapter, Jake explains that vulnerability, honesty, and having deep relationships are habits that can be practiced and learned. Do you agree with him about this? Who are the people in your life with whom you feel safe to practice being open and vulnerable?

Chapter 9

1. Take some time to journal about the idea of story. What kind of story are you living? Do you know what your life purpose is? How are

you being shaped by the circumstances of your life? How are you being shaped by your choices? What could help you live a better story?

2. How would you describe your faith life and practice before and after the divorce? Are there ways the divorce impacted your faith life for the better? For the worse?

3. What are some of the key events that have shaped your life and its direction?

4. Connor talks about being part of God's bigger story; a story that encompasses all of history and all of humanity. How does it feel to know you are part of a story that is much bigger than yourself?

Chapter 10

1. Have you ever been in a group of people who are all from divorced families? What did it feel like? If not, image what it would be like to meet with a group of people who have divorce in common. How might that shared experience impact the way you relate, speak, and connect?

2. Do you have a favourite verse or verses you go to when you need encouragement? Write out one of these verses and put it somewhere you can see it every day. A few of my favourites are:

    • Isaiah 49:15-16 *Can a woman forget her nursing child, and have no compassion on the son of her womb? Even these may forget, but I will not forget you. Behold, I have inscribed*

> *you on the palms of My hands; Your walls are continually before Me.*

- Deuteronomy 31:8 *And the LORD, He is the one who goes before you. He will be with you, He will not leave you nor forsake you; do not fear nor be dismayed.*
- Jeremiah 31:3 *The LORD appeared to him from afar, saying, "I have loved you with an everlasting love; therefore I have drawn you with lovingkindness."*
- Deuteronomy 31:6 *Be strong and courageous, do not be afraid or tremble at them, for the LORD your God is the one who goes with you. He will not fail you or forsake you.*

Chapter 11

1. Consider this quote: "*People's most basic need in life is relationship. People connected to other people thrive and grow, and those not connected wither and die. It is a medical fact, for example, that from infancy to old age, health depends on the amount of social connection people have.*" (Cloud and Townsend, *How People Grow*)
   - Make a list of the relationships in your life that **help you thrive and grow**.
   - List the relationships that **drain life from you**.
   - What changes would you like to see in your relationships?
2. In this chapter, we hear about a character named Jenny, a girl who stayed hidden in the

woods even after it was safe to come out again. What are the areas of hiding in your life? What would it look like for you to "come out of the woods"?

3. **Telling your narrative.** What is a narrative? A narrative refers to the story of your life—how the events, relationships, and patterns of thinking and relating have shaped you as an individual. The narrative takes into consideration the way you experienced and interpreted these events. Sharing your narrative is an exercise in *being known*.

   To prepare for telling your narrative, sketch a timeline of your life. Make note of significant relationships, events, conflicts, successes, failures, decisions, and opportunities. What questions, hopes, or pains were key motivators at various times of your life?

   Once you've created a timeline and considered the different elements listed above, meet with someone you trust to share your narrative. (You may find it helpful to meet with another adult child of divorce.) Give yourself 30-60 minutes to talk. You will not share every memory, but pay attention to the events, emotions, or moments that hold significance for you. If the other person would like to share his/her narrative, allow time for preparation and listen as your friend shares with you.

Chapter 12

1. Spend some time journaling about the topic of **acceptance and belonging**. When in your life

have you felt most included and part of something? What does it feel like to belong and to be wanted?

2. In this chapter, Manuel makes a comment that he spent his life protecting his parents, and therefore he found it difficult to be honest with people. What were some of the secrets you felt you had to keep as a child? Who were some of the people you felt you had to protect? Is there anything you wish you could have changed about those dynamics?

3. In this chapter, the participants reflect on a Scripture verse. What are some ways you are able to connect with God and express yourself to Him? You may want to try something different from what you're used to, such as going for a walk, drawing or colouring portions of Scripture, listening to worship music, reading poetry, journaling, writing out a prayer, or something else.

Chapter 13

1. **The Trinity** is a complex topic and one that's often overlooked, even in Christian settings. What would it look like for you to live with a deeper awareness of having been invited into the love relationship of the Trinity? Take some time to meditate on 2 Corinthians 13:14, "*The grace of the Lord Jesus Christ, and the love of God, and the fellowship of the Holy Spirit, be with you all.*" Pray or write out a response to God's invitation to relationship.

2. In this chapter, David says that God didn't create humanity out of need, but He created us to share His love with us. What's the

difference between being needed and being wanted? Which one would you rather be? What does it mean for you that God wants to be in relationship with you?

3. In this chapter, David says love always wants to give, and it always wants to serve and bless the other. How does this compare with your definition and experience of love?

Chapter 14

1. In this chapter, Katherine talks about safety. How safe did you feel as a child in terms of physical, emotional, and relational safety? How might your experience have shaped your concept of security and trust?

2. God has created us with an entire **spectrum of emotions**, yet often there are some emotions we avoid and some we are uncomfortable either expressing ourselves or seeing in others. Take a look at this list of emotions[139] and count how many of them you have experienced/expressed recently. What do you notice?

   - Happy – delighted, pleased, joyful, satisfied, thrilled, secure
   - Anxious – insecure, uneasy, restless, nauseated, tense, afraid
   - Loving – passionate, tender, comforted, sexy, assured, cozy
   - High Energy – energetic, driven, jittery, excited, playful, talkative
   - Amazed – impressed, awe, shocked, surprised, jolted, stunned
   - Confident – positive, bold, fearless, assertive, secure, self-assured

- Peaceful – comforted, relaxed, calm, protected, at ease, relieved
- Overwhelmed – burdened, distressed, paralyzed, boxed in, panicky, tense
- Traumatized – disturbed, injured, hated, damaged, unloved, shocked
- Alone – deserted, cut off, detached, abandoned, isolated, lonely
- Sad – hopeless, weepy, dejected, grieved, heavy, crushed
- Angry – hateful, bitter, irritated, grouchy, furious, provoked
- Low energy – depressed, lazy, listless, apathetic, bored, tired
- Betrayed – skeptical, duped, tricked, deceived, fooled, misled
- Confused – perplexed, dazed, mistaken, bewildered, mystified, baffled
- Ashamed – humiliated, exposed, stupid, sorry, mortified, guilty
- Despised – mocked, hated, shamed, belittled, dumb, ridiculed
- Invisible – unseen, worthless, over-looked, lost, forgotten, unknown
- Disappointed – crushed, down, frustrated, defeated, let down, distrustful

Chapter 15

1. Have you ever felt judged or looked down on because you are a child of divorce? How did you feel in that situation? Have you ever felt less than someone else because of your family

background? How do you handle/respond to those feelings?

2. Consider making a list of the romantic relationships you've had. What were some of the strengths and weaknesses of each relationship? How healthy were each of these relationships? What patterns do you notice?

3. In this chapter, David talks about the way God "hung out" with Adam and Eve in the garden of Eden in the cool of the day. What place and time is the best part of the day for you? What would it be like to picture God with you there in that place, "hanging out" with you because of the way He enjoys being with you? Take a few moments during your day today, when you are doing something you really enjoy, to imagine God is there "hanging out" with you. Respond to this experience somehow: write a poem, put on a favourite song and dance, draw something, capture the moment in a photograph, etc.

Chapter 16

1. Do you remember when/how you first learned about your parents' divorce? Who told you? What did they say? How did you respond? How did you feel? Is there anything that could have been done to help you understand or process this information in a better way? If so, what would have helped you?

2. Make a list of **lost** relationships, opportunities, possessions, freedoms, etc. Circle the three losses that have impacted you the most. Bring this list to God and let Him comfort you.

3. Use an artistic medium (drawing, painting, collaging) to creatively express your experience of the divorce.

Chapter 17

1. The artwork on the cover of the book shows a home that's been divided. The image could represent: before and after your parents' divorce; what you've experienced of home vs. what you dream of for home; different experiences of life with different parents; or something else. Take some time to draw, collage, or write about contrasting ideas of home. You could use this sentence as a starting point: "Home for me was _____, but I hope one day it will be _____."

2. Do you have difficulty piecing together or remembering parts of your childhood or family story? What are some questions you would like to ask or pieces of information you'd like to know more about?

3. In this chapter, Katherine quotes Dr. Townsend: "One of the most important processes in life is grief. God has designed grief to help us get over things." Grief isn't just about what has died, but a recognition of the good things that have been lost. In what ways has grieving allowed you to process events from your life? What are some things you may still need to grieve? You may want to do something symbolic as part of the grieving process. Some examples of ways to symbolize your grieving are having a memorial service or "funeral," writing a goodbye letter, writing a

story, creating a headstone or grave marker, sending something down a river or into the ocean, releasing balloons, etc.

4. Think about **what you need** in your life now—is it more connection with people, a way to process your grief, a deeper understanding of God's love and acceptance, or something else? Ask someone you trust to pray with you in this area.

Chapter 18

1. When you think about your childhood, what were some of the burdens you had to carry? How did it feel to have those responsibilities? Consider your current life. What burdens or expectations would you like to put down? Ask God to take them from you.

2. Consider some of the negative ideas you formed about God because of your experience of divorce. Make a list of ways your experience influences your view of God. For example: God may promise to be there for me, but I can't trust Him to keep His promises.

3. What are some positive things you've learned about God from your mother and father? For example: "My dad was willing to pick me up from any place at any time when I was a teen. From his example, I learned God is willing to give of His time and effort so I can do things I enjoy." Consider the aspects of God's character you learned from each parent. Write down some of what you have learned about God from each parent.

Chapter 19

1. **Anger** is part of the grieving process. Make a list of the healthy and unhealthy ways you deal with your anger. What stands out to you about this list?
2. What are the consequences you've seen from the unhealthy ways you (or others in your family) have dealt with anger? What advice would you give to someone in your position about finding healthier ways to deal with things?
3. In this chapter, Sloane expresses feelings of frustration and hopelessness about where she's at in life. Can you relate to any of the things she says? How do you respond to the feeling of frustration in your life?

Chapter 20

1. In this chapter, Sloane gives an illustration of the way clear water of truth and love can displace the murky water of pain and lies. What ways, people, and events bring "clear water" into your life? If you are not satisfied with the amount of good input you are receiving, where can you look for more? What changes do you need to make in order to receive more good input?
2. "Family" is a painful word for many children of divorce. "Family" is also a word that God uses to express a place of acceptance, belonging, and identity. Take a few minutes to journal about your experience of family and the conflict between what you have experienced and what family could be.

3. One idea in this chapter is that, when it comes to growth and healing in our lives, God has a part to play, and we have a part to play. How would you describe what God does in this process and what you do? Where do you see yourself trying to do too much, or too little? How can you change this?

Chapter 21

1. As you consider **the journey** Sloane and the other characters are on, which steps/scenes/emotions from the novel **do you identify with** the most? What attitudes or actions from their story would you like to implement? What do you wish you'd known earlier in life?

2. Who are the people in your life with whom you'd like to have a deeper friendship and connection? What would it look like to talk with them about this possibility?

3. Write a letter to yourself a year in the future expressing your thoughts about where you are in your journey of healing and wholeness. What hopes do you have for yourself this coming year? Comment on your relationships, emotions, expectations, or anything else that seems important.

4. What does God's invitation to "make yourselves at home in My love" sound like to you? What would it look like for you to respond to this invitation?

Afterword

1. What changes have you noticed in yourself as a result of reading this book?

2. From whom have you learned about marriage? Can you think of examples of strong, healthy marriages you'd like to learn from? Who in your circle of relationships (extended family, friends, work, church) could you observe and learn from regarding healthy marriage? Consider approaching this person/people for a conversation about marriage or to ask for input about how to have a strong marriage relationship.

3. What advice would you give to an adult child of divorce as they seek to find healing from their experience? What advice do you wish someone would have given you a year ago, five years ago, and right after the divorce? Consider writing down some pointers, as though you were coaching yourself. What advice would you give yourself?

Recipes from Aunt Vickie's Kitchen[140]

Strawberry Pie
You will need:
1 ¼ cup flour
½ cup + ⅔ cup water
1 cup + 2 tablespoons sugar
3 tablespoons cornstarch
2 pints strawberries
Whipped cream (to garnish)

Step 1:
1 ¼ cups of flour
2 tablespoons of sugar
½ cup of water
…mix together and line a pie pan. Bake at 350 degrees until golden brown.

Step 2:
Mix 1 cup of sugar together with 3 Tablespoons of cornstarch; gradually add ⅔ cup of water and 1 pint of strawberries. Cook on the stovetop until thick.

Step 3:
Put 1 pint of strawberries into the cooled pie shell, and then pour the cooked strawberry mixture over the top. Allow to cool.

Serve with whipped cream.

Key Lime Pie (Totally YUMMY!!!)
You will need:
1 14 oz. can sweetened condensed milk
3 egg yolks
2 teaspoons key lime zest (or a regular lime if key lime is not available)

½ cup key lime juice (or regular lime juice if key lime is not available)
1 9-inch graham cracker pie crust
1 cup whipping cream
3 tablespoons powdered sugar

Step 1:
Preheat the oven to 350 degrees. Whisk together the sweetened condensed milk, egg yolks, key lime zest, and key lime juice. Pour the mixture into the pie crust.

Step 2:
Bake at 350 degrees for 15 minutes, or until the pie is set. Cool completely on a wire rack. When completely cooled, chill for at least one hour before serving.

Step 3:
Beat the whipping cream on high speed with an electric mixer for 2-3 minutes until stiff peaks form, gradually adding the powdered sugar. Top each pie slice with whipped cream.

You can garnish with a lime slice.

Swedish Apple Pie
You will need:
1 9-inch unbaked pie shell
2 cups partially cooked apples
¾ cup sugar
2 teaspoons flour
⅛ teaspoon salt
1 teaspoon vanilla
1 cup dairy sour cream
1 egg

Step 1:
Combine sugar, flour, salt, and then add egg, vanilla, sour cream, and mix together. Gently stir in the apples, and then pour into the pie shell. Bake at 350 degrees for 40 minutes. Remove from the oven.

Step 2:
Combine ⅓ cup of sugar, 1 teaspoon of cinnamon, ⅓ cup of flour, and ¼ cup of butter. Sprinkle this over the top of the pie, and bake for an additional 15 minutes. Let cool before serving.

Reese's Cup Fudge
You will need:
16 Reese's cups (full-sized), chopped
3 cups chocolate chips
1 14 oz. can sweetened condensed milk

Step 1:
Line a 9x9 baking dish with parchment paper or foil. If using foil, spray with non-stick cooking pray. Set aside.

Step 2:
Add the chocolate chips and sweetened condensed milk in a pan on low-heat. Stir until the chocolate chips are melted. Stir in the chopped Reese's cups (reserving about a half cup for step 3) and allow them to melt.

Step 3:
Pour the mixture into the baking dish. Spread out to make sure it's even. Cool until room temperature. Sprinkle the reserved chopped Reese's cups on the top of the cooling fudge. Then allow it to cool in the

refrigerator for at least 2 hours. Cut into squares and serve. This yields 16-25 pieces.

Salted Caramel Mocha Fudge
You will need:
4 cups granulated sugar
1 cup skim milk
1 teaspoon pure vanilla extract
1 cup unsalted butter
1 tablespoon espresso powder
25 marshmallows, regular size
11 ½ oz. milk chocolate chips (1 package)
12 oz. semisweet chocolate chips (1 package)
2 oz. unsweetened chocolate
1 11 oz. bag caramel bits, or about 2 cups caramels
2 tablespoons heavy cream
1 tablespoon kosher salt

Directions:
In a large saucepan, combine sugar, milk, vanilla, butter, and espresso powder. Bring to a boil over medium high heat, stirring constantly. Once boiling, keep at a rolling boil for two full minutes (still stirring).

(For this next step, I use a stand mixer with whisk attachment, but a hand mixer would work, too.)

In a large bowl, combine marshmallows and chocolate. Pour hot mixture over these ingredients and blend until smooth. I turn my mixer on medium speed and allow it to blend for about 2-3 minutes, scraping down the sides of the bowl several times.

While this is mixing, place your caramel and heavy cream in a microwave-safe bowl and heat for 1-2 minutes, stirring every 30 seconds until melted and smooth. Set aside.

Pour the creamy fudge mixture into a parchment-paper-lined 15x10x1 baking sheet. Drizzle with hot caramel, using a knife to swirl it into the fudge. Sprinkle immediately with kosher salt (or coarse sea salt). Refrigerate for 4 hours, or overnight. Cut into small bites and store in the refrigerator for up to two weeks. ENJOY!

Fanny Farmer Fudge (a true classic!)
You will need:
2 cups sugar
⅔ cup evaporated milk
½ cup butter
1 cup semisweet chocolate chips
1 teaspoon real vanilla extract
1 cup chopped walnuts (optional)

Step 1:
Butter an 8x8x2 or 9x9x2 square pan.

Step 2:
In a medium-sized saucepan, combine sugar and milk. Heat to boiling, stirring constantly. Boil for 5 minutes, counting time from when the rolling boil was first reached (a continuous boil). Remove from heat and stir in butter and chocolate chips until well blended. Stir in the vanilla and walnuts, then beat one minute.

Step 3:
Pour into the buttered pan. Allow to cool, then transfer to the refrigerator. Let fudge harden. Cut into squares.

Yields 16-25 pieces.

Lemon Gelato
You will need:
6 lemons, zested & juiced (approx. ½ cup lemon zest & 1 cup lemon juice—save the lemon halves to use as serving dishes!)
6 egg yolks
1 ¼ cups heavy whipping cream
2 ½ cups half and half
½ teaspoon pure vanilla extract
1 ¼ cups sugar

What to do:
Whisk your egg yolks and heavy cream together in a bowl & set aside. Into a large saucepan, add half and half, lemon zest, and sugar. Heat over medium heat, stirring frequently until sugar dissolves. Remove from heat. Add some of the warm half and half mixture to the egg yolk mixture into order to temper.
GRADUALLY add the egg yolk mixture into the half and half mixture and stir well to combine. Return to medium heat and cook until mixture thickens. Remove from heat and stir in vanilla extract.

Allow pan to cool slightly; cover with saran wrap and place into the fridge to cool completely. When you're ready to make your gelato, stir in the lemon juice and follow instructions on your gelato maker. Serve this in cleaned-out lemon halves!

Toasted Coconut Gelato
You will need:
2 cups + 3 tablespoons whole milk
1 ¾ cups coconut milk
1 cup loosely packed toasted unsweetened coconut
flakes, plus additional for garnish
½ cup sugar
1 teaspoon coconut extract
1 teaspoon vanilla extract
1 tablespoon cornstarch
Pinch salt

Instructions:
In a heavy saucepot, add 2 cups of milk, coconut milk,
sugar, and salt. Bring to a low boil on medium-low
heat. Be careful not to scorch. With the remaining
milk, add cornstarch to make a slurry. When milk and
coconut milk come to a boil, add the slurry and
extracts. Cook on low and whisk often so that clumps
do not form. The mixture is cooked when you can run
a line on the back of a spoon without the mixture
coming back together.

Cool the mixture to room temperature and then chill in
the refrigerator for a minimum of 12 hours. Add the
mixture to your ice cream maker and follow the
manufacturer's directions. When half the time has
elapsed, slowly add the toasted coconut, allowing it to
be thoroughly incorporated into the mixture.

Transfer to a storage container and freeze until desired
firmness. Before serving, allow the gelato to sit on
your counter for a few minutes for a better texture,
making it easier to scoop. Serve with a sprinkle of
toasted coconut flakes.

Endnotes

1   Jen Abbas, *Generation Ex: Adult Children of Divorce and the Healing of Our Pain.* (Colorado Springs, CO: Waterbrook, 2004), 12.

2   Andrew Root, *The Children of Divorce: The Loss of Family as the Loss of Being.* (Grand Rapids, MI: Baker Academic, 2010), xvi.

3   Abbas, *Generation Ex,* 182-183.

4   Judith Wallerstein, Julia Lewis, and Sandra Blakeslee, *The Unexpected Legacy of Divorce.* (New York, NY: Hyperion, 2000), xxxiii.

5   Ibid., 62.

6   Elizabeth Marquardt, *Between Two Worlds: The Inner Lives of Children of Divorce.* (New York, NY: Three Rivers Press, 2005), 32.

7   "One-quarter of today's young adults are grown children of divorce. How this generation approaches questions of moral and spiritual meaning—and what choices they make for themselves and their families with regard to religious identity and involvement—will undoubtedly influence broader trends in the churches." Elizabeth Marquardt, Amy Ziettlow, and Charles E. Stokes, *Does the Shape of Families Shape Faith?: Challenging the Churches to Confront the Impact of Family Change.* (New York, NY: Institute for American Values, 2013), 10.

8   Ibid., 11.

9   Wallerstein, Lewis, and Blakeslee, *Unexpected Legacy,* 299-300.

10   Curt Thompson, *Anatomy of the Soul: Surprising
     Connections Between Neuroscience and Spiritual
     Practices That Can Transform Your Life and
     Relationships*. (Carrollton, TX: SaltRiver, 2010),
     xiv.

11   Wallerstein, Lewis, and Blakeslee, *Unexpected
     Legacy*, 37.

12   Wallerstein, Lewis, and Blakeslee, *Unexpected
     Legacy*, xxix.

13   Ibid., 27.

14   Marquardt, *Between Two Worlds,* 101.

15   Ibid., 60-61.

16   Marquardt, Ziettlow, and Stokes, *Does the Shape
     of Families Shape Faith?,* 15.

17   Wallerstein, Lewis, and Blakeslee, *Unexpected
     Legacy*, 159.

18   Marquardt, Ziettlow, and Stokes, *Does the Shape
     of Families Shape Faith?,* 12.

19   The idea of a panel discussion for children of
     divorce is from the book *Does the Shape of
     Families Shape Faith?*

20   Abbas, *Generation Ex,* 12.

21   Ibid., 90.

22   Marquardt, *Between Two Worlds,* 31.

23   Root, *Children,* 85.

24   Andrew Root's book looks extensively at the
     question of ontology (*being*). "Parents can assure
     the child repeatedly that they both (now
     individually) love her, but that is not her concern;
     she does not doubt this. Rather, she doubts who

she is and whether she can be at all, now that there
is no longer unity in the community of history
responsible for her being." Ibid., 116.

25   Ibid., 114.

26   "When they reach their eighteenth birthday, many
young adults in divorced families feel like second-
class citizens. That's when the last child support
check arrives and that's when they realize how
disadvantaged they are compared to their friends
in intact families… A little less than 30 percent of
the youngsters from divorced families received
full or consistently partial support for college
compared with almost 90 percent of youngsters in
intact families. That's a whopping difference that
speaks volumes about how children of divorce
lead an entirely different life compared to their
next-door neighbors in intact families."
Wallerstein, Lewis, and Blakeslee, *Unexpected
Legacy*, 248-249.

27   Marquardt, *Between Two Worlds,* 59.

28   Wallerstein, Lewis, and Blakeslee, *Unexpected
Legacy*, 21.

29   Michael P. Nichols, *The Lost Art of Listening.*
(New York, NY: Gilford Press, 2009), 248.

30   Ibid., 254.

31   Mark 14:32-41.

32   "If, however, you encounter a therapist or a good
friend who, when you feel sad, responds with
empathy and comfort, your memory of the feeling
of sadness will change, even if ever so little at
first. You will not have changed the facts of your

past, but you will change your memory of it."
Thompson, *Anatomy of the Soul,* 78.

³³ Abbas, *Generation Ex,* 118-119.

³⁴ John Townsend, *Hiding From Love: How to Change the Withdrawal Patterns That Isolate and Imprison You*. (Grand Rapids, MI: Zondervan, 1991), 64-65.

³⁵ Ibid., 64-65.

³⁶ Wallerstein, Lewis, and Blakeslee, *Unexpected Legacy*, 298.

³⁷ Abbas, *Generation Ex,* 12.

³⁸ Specifically chapter 7: Attachment: The Connections of Life. pp.109-134. Thompson, *Anatomy of the Soul.*

³⁹ "In other words, the way people learn to manage emotional states as children will follow them into their adult friendships, marriages, and work relationships." Ibid., 116.

⁴⁰ Ibid., 119.

⁴¹ "…attachment patterns can be changed, even in adulthood. Through a process called earned secure attachment, people can develop the sense of well-being and confidence that results from healthy attachment. In other words, they can finally tell their life story in a coherent, complete way. It won't happen, though, simply because they take in new factual information or have strong willpower. This transformation requires either a significant encounter with an outside relationship or a profound change in circumstances." Ibid., 136.

⁴² Ibid., 133.

43   Root, *Children,* 125.

44   Ibid., 96.

45   Retrieved from: http://www.children-and-divorce.com/children-divorce-statistics.html.

46   Marquardt, *Between Two Worlds,* 178-179.

47   William J. Doherty and Leah Ward Sears, "Delaying divorce to save marriages." *The Washington Post*, Oct. 20, 2011. Retrieved from https://www.washingtonpost.com/opinions/delaying-divorce-to-save-marriages/2011/10/19/gIQAKh0f1L_story.html

48   Ibid.

49   James A. K. Smith, *Imagining the Kingdom: How Worship Works*. (Grand Rapids, MI: Baker Academic, 2010), 108.

50   Donald Miller, *A Million Miles in a Thousand Years: How I Learned to Live a Better Story*. (Nashville, TN: Thomas Nelson, 2009).

51   Marquardt, *Between Two Worlds,* 139.

52   Wallerstein, Lewis, and Blakeslee, *Unexpected Legacy*, 298.

53   Abbas, *Generation Ex,* 118.

54   Cloud & Townsend, *How People Grow,* 92.

55   Ephesians 1:11. The Message.

56   "The relational community of Father, Son, and Spirit is not simply an organization constructed around tasks. It is not a committee called together simply to do things… Rather, the inner life of the Trinity is a unit, and the fabric of the unity of inner relation of Father, Son, and Spirit is love… It is

relational love that leads to creation..." Root, *Children,* 79.

[57] Hebrews 2:8. "YOU HAVE PUT ALL THINGS IN SUBJECTION UNDER HIS FEET. For in subjecting all things to him, He left nothing that is not subject to him. But now we do not yet see all things subjected to him." New American Standard Bible.

[58] 1 John 3:2. "Beloved, now we are children of God, and it has not appeared as yet what we will be. We know that when He appears, we will be like Him, because we will see Him just as He is." New American Standard Bible.

[59] 1 Corinthians 13:12. "For now we see in a mirror dimly, but then face to face; now I know in part, but then I will know fully, just as I also have been fully known." New American Standard Bible.

[60] Ephesians 1:11. The Message.

[61] Cloud & Townsend, *How People Grow,* 122.

[62] "(Rejection) changes us. It makes us guarded and tentative, even suspicious, and we go into hiding. Why does rejection hurt us so deeply? The power of rejection comes from the way we are wired. We are made for acceptance... As a fish thrives and flourishes in water, human beings thrive and flourish in acceptance. It is our native environment. We are not much good, and certainly not happy, without it." Baxter Kruger, *The Parable of the Dancing God.* (Downers Grove, IL: InterVarsity Press), 6.

[63] Townsend, *Hiding From Love,* 17-28.

[64] Townsend, *Hiding From Love,* 153-154.

[65] Ibid., 40.

[66] Marquardt, Ziettlow, and Stokes, *Does the Shape of Families Shape Faith?*, 25-26.

[67] Thompson, *Anatomy of the Soul*, 23.

[68] Cloud & Townsend, *How People Grow,* 30.

[69] Wallerstein, Lewis, and Blakeslee, *Unexpected Legacy*, 305.

[70] See The Bible Project's five-minute video on what it means to be made in the image of God: https://www.youtube.com/watch?v=YbipxLDtY8c

[71] Dallas Willard, *The Divine Conspiracy: Rediscovering Our Hidden Life in God.* (New York, NY: HarperSanFrancisco, 1998), 62.

[72] Matthew 3:17. "And behold, a voice out of the heavens said, 'This is My beloved Son, in whom I am well-pleased.'" New American Standard Bible.

[73] Luke 9:35. "Then a voice came out of the cloud, saying, 'This is My Son, My Chosen One; listen to Him!'" New American Standard Bible.

[74] John 14:2. "In My Father's house are many dwelling places; if it were not so, I would have told you; for I go to prepare a place for you." New American Standard Bible.

[75] Matthew 6:9-13. "Pray, then, in this way:

'Our Father who is in heaven,
Hallowed be Your name.
Your kingdom come.
Your will be done
On earth as it is in heaven.
Give us this day our daily bread.

And forgive us our debts, as we also have forgiven
our debtors.
And do not lead us into temptation, but deliver us
from evil.
For Yours is the kingdom and the power and the
glory forever. Amen.'" New American
Standard Bible.

[76] John 16:13 "But when He, the Spirit of truth,
comes, He will guide you into all the truth; for He
will not speak on His own initiative, but whatever
He hears, He will speak; and He will disclose to
you what is to come." New American Standard
Bible.

[77] Julie Canlis speaks about the unity and distinctness
of the Trinity in her lecture series "The Relational
Self: Trinitarian Insights on What it Means to Be
Human." Regent College Audio, 2010.

[78] Wallerstein, Lewis, and Blakeslee, *Unexpected
Legacy*, 62.

[79] Maslow's hierarchy of needs is a theory proposed
in 1943 by Abraham Maslow. It describes factors
necessary for growth and development. The
foundational need is physiological, followed by
safety and security, love and belonging, self-
esteem, and finally self-actualization. When lower
needs are not met, he theorized that it is difficult or
impossible to progress farther up the pyramid.
Retrieved from:
http://www.researchhistory.org/2012/06/16/maslo
ws-hierarchy-of-needs/

[80] "Tragically, it is well documented that children are
at significantly greater risk of abuse after their
parents' divorce... anywhere from one-third to
one-half—of girls with divorced parents report

having been molested or sexually abused as children, most often by their mothers' boyfriends or stepfathers." Marquardt, *Between Two Worlds,* 60-61.

[81] See chapter 3, Training vs. Trying, in John Ortberg, *The Life You've Always Wanted: Spiritual Disciplines for Ordinary People.* (Grand Rapids, MI: Zondervan).

[82] To listen to Dave Brubeck's "Take Five" (written and recorded in 1959), check out the YouTube video: https://www.youtube.com/watch?v=PHdU5sHigYQ

[83] I don't know if John Ortberg has a video specifically about the concept of training vs. trying, but I would gladly watch one if it existed!

[84] "…if you do not attend to categorical emotions like joy, anger, and shame, your relationship with God will be limited. Not only will you be unable to share your feelings with Him, but you'll be functionally disconnected from His feelings." Thompson, *Anatomy of the Soul,* 105.

[85] Ibid., 95-96.

[86] Root, *Children,* 54-55.

[87] "Once we felt so much loss, so many times, many of us grew numb to it." Marquardt, *Between Two Worlds,* 173.

[88] Root, *Children,* 136.

[89] Marquardt, *Between Two Worlds,* 168.

[90] Wallerstein, Lewis, and Blakeslee, *Unexpected Legacy,* 298.

[91] Ibid., xxxv.

[92] Ibid., xxxv.

[93] Genesis 3:8. This verse describes the day Adam and Eve ate from the tree of the knowledge of good and evil and hid themselves from God. God is described as walking in the garden in the cool of the day, calling out for Adam and Eve when they are hiding from His presence.

[94] Ibid., 32.

[95] "You did not experience the fullness of what God designed for you in a family, and so you *have* been hurt. It's just that you are part of a generation that has learned to see these scars as normal." Abbas, *Generation Ex,* 2.

[96] "Children are vulnerable after a divorce and—especially if there is a history of abuse, addiction, or mental illness in the family—they can be easy prey for abusers. As we've seen, children of divorce are left alone much more often than other children are. Many are too accessible to adults with bad intentions, especially to men who enter the home as a mother's boyfriend or new husband." Marquardt, *Between Two Worlds,* 63.

[97] "Rather, they say flatly, 'The day my parents divorced is the day my childhood ended.'" Wallerstein, Lewis, and Blakeslee, *Unexpected Legacy*, 26.

[98] Abbas, *Generation Ex,* 45.

[99] Cloud & Townsend, *How People Grow,* 135.

[100] "Before we can have peaceful hearts, we must grieve our disappointments and hurts. We must give ourselves permission to let the tears flow.

Perhaps we see tears as an indication of weakness or a loss of control, and we want nothing more than to be strong and self-sufficient. Understand that grief comes in waves. We can't 'get over' our loss in one or two crying sessions. We may grieve for years as new experiences reveal new losses—and that's okay… The only way to deal with loss is to go through it." Abbas, *Generation Ex,* 32-33.

101 Cloud & Townsend, *How People Grow,* 231.

102 Wallerstein, Lewis, and Blakeslee, *Unexpected Legacy,* 47.

103 These quotes are based on answers to a survey I created during my research for this book.

104 "Dad's first marriage is a skeleton in their Cleaver family closet. After nearly twenty-five years, Joyce [the stepmom] still seems to struggle with the fact that Dad was married to someone else before he was married to her. And now what has evolved is that my brother and I have no defined identity within his second family. We aren't peers to our half-siblings, nor are we authority figures. We are electrons, forever destined to orbit their family nucleus." Root, *Children,* 41-42.

105 Thoughts on Jewish funerals and mourning taken from Lauren F. Winner, *Mudhouse Sabbath: An Invitation to a Life of Spiritual Discipline.* (Brewster, MA: Paraclete Press, 2003.)

106 Cloud & Townsend, *How People Grow,* 233.

107 Ibid., 233.

108 This conversation is based on a conversation with Andrea Yeung, Pastor/Director of Healing Ministries at Tenth Church, Vancouver, Canada.

[109] Matthew 11:28-30 "Come to Me, all who are weary and heavy-laden, and I will give you rest. Take My yoke upon you and learn from Me, for I am gentle and humble in heart, and YOU WILL FIND REST FOR YOUR SOULS. For My yoke is easy and My burden is light." New American Standard Bible.

[110] Paraphrased from Dennis Linn, *Sleeping with Bread: Holding What Gives You Life.* (Paulist Press, 2002).

[111] "We, especially we Protestants, have a built-in allergy to repetition in worship, thought we are quite happy to affirm the value of repetition in almost every other sphere of life, from study to music to sports to art." Smith, *Imagining the Kingdom,* 181.

[112] "And herein lies a central aspect of Christian worship: it is an alternative imaginary, a way that the Spirit of God invites us into the Story of God in Christ reconciling the world to Himself. But as we've seen, if such a Story is really going to capture our imaginations, it needs to get into our gut—it needs to be written on our hearts. And the way to the heart is through the body." Ibid., 150.

[113] Credit to Maureen Menard for creating this assignment for the Master's program.

[114] "Christian worship is an intentionally decentering practice, calling us out of ourselves into the very life of God. That worship begins with a *call* is already a first displacement that is at the same time an invitation: to find ourselves *in* Christ… the practices of Christian worship are fundamentally ecstatic—calling us out of ourselves and into the life of the Triune God, not to 'lose' ourselves, but

[115] Icheon Master Hand/Lee Hyuang Gu, https://www.youtube.com/watch?v=xDmBtNrC5Lc.

to be found in him." Smith, *Imagining the Kingdom,* 149.

[116] For an interesting look at the roles of the disciple, God, and the discipler in the process of growth and development, see Cloud & Townsend, *How People Grow.*

[117] Ibid., 35.

[118] Nichols, *The Lost Art of Listening*, 181-182.

[119] Townsend, *Hiding From Love,* 62.

[120] "It's estimated that one million children in the US alone experience the divorce of their parents each year. Globally the number is much higher." Marquardt, Ziettlow, and Stokes, *Does the Shape of Families Shape Faith?,* 10.

[121] The dialogue between Amy and Sloane is based on a conversation I had with Miranda Heathcote beside a river in Spain in June 2015.

[122] "Repairing bonding deficits involves two factors. First, it requires finding safe, warm relationships in which emotional needs will be accepted and loved, not criticized and judged... Second, repair requires taking risks with our needs. This means taking a step of humility. It means bringing our loneliness and abandoned feelings to other believers..." Townsend, *Hiding From Love,* 70.

[123] Cloud & Townsend, *How People Grow,* 96.

[124] Ibid., 157.

[125] 2 Corinthians 5:17-20. "Therefore if anyone is in Christ, he is a new creature; the old things passed away; behold, new things have come. Now all these things are from God, who reconciled us to Himself through Christ and gave us the ministry of reconciliation, namely, that God was in Christ reconciling the world to Himself, not counting their trespasses against them, and He has committed to us the word of reconciliation. Therefore, we are ambassadors for Christ, as though God were making an appeal through us; we beg you on behalf of Christ, be reconciled to God." New American Standard Bible.

[126] "What we do is driven by who we are, by the kind of person we have become. And that shaping of our character is, to a great extent, the effect of stories that have captivated us, that have sunk into our bones—stories that 'picture' what we think life is about, what constitutes 'the good life.' We live *into* stories we've absorbed; we become characters in the drama that has captivated us." Smith, *Imagining the Kingdom,* 32.

[127] "If you are going to help people grow, you *must* understand the necessity of relationship for growth. Often people in the church who are teaching others how to grow eliminate the role of the Body. In fact, sometimes these people teach that their students don't need people at all, that Christ alone is sufficient, or that His Word or prayer is enough. They actively and directly lead others to not depend on people at all." Cloud & Townsend, *How People Grow,* 121.

[128] "For the child was created and made real not from the choice of one, but from the union of the love or a relational community. Therefore, often what

children grieve is not the loss of love directed toward them, but the loss of the mysterious and powerful community of love that existed before them and elected to invite them into the world." Root, *Children,* 81.

[129] The book of Ephesians uses five metaphors to describe the church. *Family* and *body* are two of them. Can you find the other three?

[130] "...one of the most painful aspects of divorce is that it punctures one's story. After the divorce, or as we age and come to grips with the divorce, it is ever harder to construct a clear narrative of the relationships and events that brought us into the world. There persists a feeling of being disconnected, not only from ourselves, but from history itself." Root, *Children,* 131.

[131] Luke 15:11-24.

[132] To learn more about adoption in ancient Rome, check out: http://www.quodlibet.net/articles/murray-adoption.shtml

[133] Ephesians 1 talks about adoption into God's family and the inheritance we have as his children. See also Romans 8:15 and Galatians 4:5.

[134] From *The Message.*

[135] This is a sample of questions used in a weekly accountability email.

Checking-in questions for the past week:

1. In what ways have you nurtured/invested in your relationship with God?
2. Where have you experienced God's love and care for you?

3. What's your emotional state?
4. Have you been exposed to sexually alluring material or entertained inappropriate thoughts about someone who is not your spouse?
5. Have you lacked integrity in your financial dealings this week, or coveted something that does not belong to you?
6. Have you been honoring, understanding, and generous in your important relationships?
7. Have you damaged another person by your words, either behind their back or face-to-face?
8. Have you been completely honest with me?

136 Root, *Children,* 122.

137 John 14:1-3. New American Standard Bible.

138 John 15:9. The Message.

139 This list of feeling words was taken from the website howwelove.com. They have other free resources related to listening, emotional awareness, and healthy relating (https://s3.amazonaws.com/hwl-prod-assets/uploads/2012/05/16030007/SoulWordList.pdf).

140 Recipes courtesy of Vickie Hedgepeth.

Made in the USA
Columbia, SC
29 March 2018